Collins

Work on your
Idioms

Sandra Anderson & Cheryl Pelteret

Collins

HarperCollins Publishers
77-85 Fulham Palace Road
Hammersmith
London W6 8JB

First edition 2012

Reprint 10 9 8 7 6 5 4 3 2 1 0

© HarperCollins Publishers 2012

ISBN 978-0-00-746467-8

Collins® is a registered trademark of HarperCollins Publishers Limited

www.collinselt.com

A catalogue record for this book is available from the British Library

Typeset in India by Aptara

Printed in China by South China Printing Co.

About the authors

Sandra Anderson is a lexicographer and ELT author based in the UK. She taught English to international students in the UK, in Europe and in Asia for ten years, and then used that classroom experience to inform her work on dictionaries and language learning materials, concentrating especially on grammar and vocabulary development.

Cheryl Pelteret has been involved in language teaching for the past 30 years – as a teacher, editor and writer. She has taught students of all ages and levels in the UK and in Turkey, and has written several course books and a range of supplementary materials for adults, teenagers and young learners. Cheryl is the author of *English for Life: Speaking* (Collins, 2012).

Contents

How to use this book

Welcome to *Work on your Idioms!*

Who is this book for?

The book is suitable for:

- intermediate to advanced learners
- learners who are CEF (Common European Framework) level B1+.

You can use the book:

- as a self-study course
- as supplementary material on a general English course.

Book structure

Work on your Idioms contains:

- 25 units covering over 300 of the most common idioms
- a comprehensive answer key
- appendices which include: a study guide with tips to help you remember idioms and use them correctly, and a section covering American English versions of the idioms in the units
- an index to help you find idioms quickly and easily.

Idioms are figurative phrases that exist in all languages. They have a literal meaning, but they also have a figurative meaning, which is not always obvious. They form an important part of everyone's vocabulary and are used both in formal and informal language. They are, however, much more common in informal, spoken English. They should not be confused with slang, which is very often inappropriate in certain social situations.

The idioms in this book are grouped by topic to make them easier to remember and to help you use and understand them in everyday situations. The idioms are presented alphabetically and in large bold type over two pages in each unit, so that you can see them clearly and find them easily.

Unit structure

Each unit is presented over four pages. The first two pages of each unit present the idioms, together with full sentence definitions, examples, and notes. The second two pages provide exercises to help you practise using the idioms. Each unit is self-contained, so you can study the units in any order, by selecting the topic you want to study.

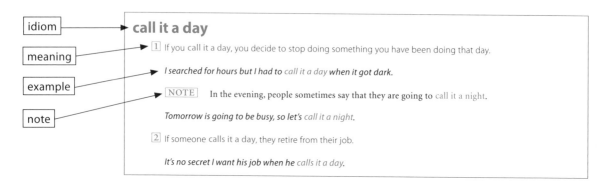

Definitions

The definitions of idioms are given in full sentences in simple, natural English.

Examples

Each definition is followed by at least one example. All of the examples are taken from the Collins Corpus, a huge database of real language from a variety of sources. The examples have been carefully chosen to show common patterns and typical uses of the idiom, so that you can see how it is really used in English today.

Notes

Notes give you extra information, for example, information about the idiom's origin and any particularly difficult or unusual vocabulary in it.

British and American English

Most of the idioms in this book are used in both British and American English. However, there are sometimes cases where an idiom has an American English variation. There is a section at the back of the book covering the American English versions of these idioms.

Exercises

Each unit contains six exercises designed to help you practise using all the idioms from the unit. The examples used in the exercises will help you to understand the idioms in context and help you to be more confident about using them correctly. You will find answers to all the exercises in the Answer key at the back of the book.

Your turn!

In addition to the exercises, each unit contains a **Your turn!** activity. These are designed to help you use the idioms to talk about your own ideas or experiences.

Other titles

Also available in this range are:

- *Work on your Accent*
- *Work on your Phrasal Verbs*

Knowledge and understanding

get the hang of something

If you get the hang of an activity, you learn how to do it well. [INFORMAL]

After a few months you will start getting the hang of the language and expressing yourself quite well.

get the picture

If you get the picture, you understand what is happening in a situation. [INFORMAL]

NOTE   This expression is often used when someone does not understand something immediately.

Anna was giggling. She was beginning to get the picture.

get the wrong end of the stick or get hold of the wrong end of the stick

If someone gets the wrong end of the stick or gets hold of the wrong end of the stick, they completely misunderstand a situation or something that is said. [INFORMAL]

Did I get hold of the wrong end of the stick? Was that not what he meant?

get your head around something or get your head round something

If you get your head around a fact or an idea, you succeed in understanding it or accepting it. [BRITISH, INFORMAL]

At first people laughed at me because they simply could not get their head around what I was telling them.

It's hard to get your head round figures this big.

go in one ear and out the other

If something that you tell someone goes in one ear and out the other, they pay no attention to it, or forget about it immediately.

I've told him so many times – it just goes in one ear and out the other.

a grey area

If you call something a grey area, you mean that it is unclear, for example because nobody is sure how to deal with it, or it falls between two separate categories of things.

Tabloid papers paint all sportsmen as heroes or villains. There is no grey area in between.

not have a clue

If you do not have a clue about something, you do not know anything about it, or you have no idea what to do about it. [INFORMAL]

I don't have a clue what I'm supposed to be doing.

jump to conclusions

If someone jumps to conclusions, they decide too quickly that something is true, when they do not know all the facts.

Forgive me. I thought you were married. I shouldn't jump to conclusions.

NOTE   You can also say that someone jumps to a/the conclusion.

I didn't want her to jump to the conclusion that the divorce was in any way her fault.

NOTE   People sometimes use leap instead of jump.

The medical establishment was careful not to leap to conclusions.

put two and two together

If you put two and two together, you correctly guess the truth about something from the information that you have.

He put two and two together and guessed what the police were searching for.

NOTE   You can say that someone puts two and two together and makes five, to mean that they guess something more exciting or interesting than the truth.

Mr Lane's solicitor said that the police had put two and two together and made five.

read between the lines

If you read between the lines, you understand what someone really means, or what is really happening in a situation, even though it is not stated openly.

He didn't go into details, but reading between the lines it appears that he was forced to leave.

NOTE   You can also talk about what is between the lines.

He didn't give a reason, but I sensed something between the lines.

take something on board

If you take an idea, suggestion, or fact on board, you understand it or accept it. [BRITISH]

NOTE   The literal meaning of this expression is to take something onto a boat or ship.

I listened to them, took their comments on board, and then made the decision.

up to speed

If you are up to speed, you have all the latest information about something.

We try to keep people entertained and up to speed with what's going on in town.

NOTE   You can say that you bring someone up to speed, or that they get up to speed when you give them all the latest information about something.

I guess I should bring you up to speed on what's been happening since I came to see you yesterday. The president has been getting up to speed on foreign policy.

Exercise 1

Complete the sentences with the words in the box.

| ear | clue | hang | picture | stick | area |

1 I soon began to get the _____ of the new filing system.
2 Anna doesn't have a _____ how to talk to children.
3 The difference between telling a lie and not telling the whole truth is a grey _____.
4 I thought she was paying for dinner but I must have got the wrong end of the _____.
5 Brad tried to remember the directions but they seemed to have gone in one _____ and out the other.
6 The inspector spent a few minutes with the victim and soon began to get the _____.

Exercise 2

Match sentence halves 1–6 with A–F to make complete sentences.

1 We saw them together in the restaurant and it was so easy to

2 I've told them I'm a vegetarian many times but they just don't

3 The real skill of being an agony aunt is being able to

4 I've learnt a lot about the new regulations and I'll run a training day to

5 The international dateline is an idea I've never been able to

6 Unfortunately, the children were disappointed; they

A read between the lines.

B take it on board.

C had put two and two together and made five.

D jump to conclusions.

E get my head around.

F bring you all up to speed.

Exercise 3

Complete the sentences. Choose the best answers.

1 Then you click 'save' and move the file to here. Do you *read between the lines / get the picture / put two and two together*?
2 It's going to take me a couple of days to get *up to speed / the picture / the wrong end of the stick* with the new project.
3 This is a very difficult exercise. I just can't *jump to conclusions / go in one ear and out the other / get my head round it*.
4 Don't worry. You'll soon *get the hang of it / jump to conclusions / get the wrong end of the stick*.
5 Listen to all the evidence and don't *take it on board / jump to conclusions / get your head around it*.
6 Adam shook his head; he didn't *put two and two together / read between the lines / have a clue* how to fix this.

Exercise 4

Replace the underlined words with the correct idioms in the box.

| get hold of the wrong end of the stick | get the hang of it | get the picture |
| go in one ear and out the other | haven't got a clue | read between the lines |

1 You don't have to explain it anymore. I understand the situation.
2 He doesn't listen carefully, and tends to misunderstand.
3 I don't think I'll be able to do the accounts. I know nothing about book keeping.
4 They haven't actually said anything is wrong, but I can sense it.
5 It's difficult at first, but after a bit of practice, you learn how to do it.
6 You have to repeat everything to them. Whatever you say will be forgotten immediately afterwards!

Work on your Idioms Knowledge and understanding

Exercise 5

Use sentences A–F to answer questions 1–6.

1 Whose company has adopted a new way of working?

2 Who is surprised at how strict his working conditions are becoming?

3 Who thinks he will soon have a new boss?

4 Who is improving his expertise at work?

5 Who is expecting to benefit from recent events?

6 Who wants to work for a different company?

A Veejay feels he hasn't a clue how to find a better employer.

B Nik is getting himself up to speed on the new tax law.

C Khalid leapt to the conclusion that the CEO would now resign.

D Stefan's firm has really taken the idea of teleworking on board.

E Cheng put two and two together and hoped this would mean a promotion for him.

F Xavier can't get his head around all the new rules in the office.

Exercise 6

Complete the table. Put the idioms in the correct groups.

not have a clue	get your head around something	get the wrong end of the stick	a grey area
up to speed	take something on board	read between the lines	jump to conclusions
get the hang of something	get the picture	put two and two together	go in one ear and out the other

understanding correctly	1 _____
	2 _____
	3 _____
	4 _____
	5 _____
	6 _____
	7 _____
not understanding	1 _____
	2 _____
	3 _____
	4 _____
	5 _____

Your turn!

Think about learning experiences you or people around you have had recently. Use the idioms in this unit to talk about them. For example:

I finally managed to get my head around *how a car engine works.*

My parents still haven't got the hang of *text messaging.*

The assistant chef had **got the wrong end of the stick**

2

Memory and mind

bear something in mind or keep something in mind

If you tell someone to bear something in mind or keep something in mind, you are reminding or warning them about something important which they should remember.

There are a few general rules to bear in mind when selecting plants.

Keep in mind that some places are more dangerous than others for women travelling alone.

cross your mind

If something crosses your mind, you suddenly think of it.

It crossed my mind that she might be lying about her age.

food for thought

If something gives you food for thought, it makes you think very hard about an issue.

This Italian trip gave us all much food for thought.

a gut reaction

A gut reaction is a reaction that you have immediately and strongly, without thinking about something or being aware of your reasons.

NOTE   The gut is the tube inside the body through which food passes while it is being digested.

My immediate gut reaction was to never write again.

lose the plot

If someone loses the plot, they become confused or crazy, or no longer know how to deal with a situation. [INFORMAL]

NOTE   A plot is the sequence of events in a story.

Vikram's working so many hours that he's losing the plot – he's making mistakes and keeps falling asleep on the job.

miles away

If someone is miles away, they are completely unaware of what is happening or of what someone is saying, because they are thinking deeply about something else.

You didn't hear a word I said, did you? You were miles away.

a mind like a sieve

If you have a mind like a sieve or a brain like a sieve, you have a bad memory and often forget things.

He's lost his keys again – he's got a mind like a sieve.

NOTE   You can use brain instead of mind and you can say is like a sieve instead of have.

He lost his car keys but admitted that his brain was like a sieve.

off the top of your head

If you say that you are commenting on something off the top of your head, you mean that what you are about to say is an immediate reaction and is not a carefully considered opinion, and so it might not be correct. [SPOKEN]

I can't remember off the top of my head which plan they used, but it certainly wasn't this one.

off your head

If you say that someone is off their head or out of their head, you mean that they are very strange, foolish, or dangerous. [BRITISH, INFORMAL]

It's like working in a war zone. You must be off your head to live in that area.

on the tip of your tongue

1 If a remark or question is on the tip of your tongue, you want to say it, but stop yourself.

It was on the tip of my tongue to tell him he'd have to ask Charlie. But I said nothing.

2 If something such as a word, answer, or name is on the tip of your tongue, you know it and can almost remember it, but not quite.

I know this, no, no, don't tell me … oh, it's on the tip of my tongue!

out of your mind

1 If you say that someone is out of their mind, you mean that they are crazy or stupid. [INFORMAL]

You spent five hundred pounds on a jacket! Are you out of your mind?

2 If you are out of your mind with worry, grief, fear, etc., you are extremely worried, sad, afraid, etc.

She's out of her mind with worry; her husband left the hotel yesterday and hasn't been seen since.

NOTE   You can also say that someone is going out of their mind.

I was so sure that was what she said. Sometimes I wonder if I'm going out of my mind.

We have a lot of problems in our family. I'm going out of my mind with the worry of it all.

rack your brain

If you rack your brain, you think very hard about something or try very hard to remember it.

They asked me for fresh ideas, so I racked my brain, but couldn't come up with anything.

NOTE   You can also say rack your brains.

Alma racked her brains for something to say.

NOTE   The old-fashioned spelling wrack is occasionally used instead of rack in this expression. *Bob was wracking his brain, trying to think where he had seen the man before.*

ring a bell

If something rings a bell, it is slightly familiar to you and you know you have heard it before, but you do not remember it fully.

The name rings a bell but I can't think where I've heard it.

Exercise 1

Complete the sentences with the words in the box. Some of the sentences have more than one answer.

head | mind | brain | thought | brains

1 Do you have the memory of an elephant or a _____ like a sieve?
2 You are mad. Totally, completely and utterly off your _____.
3 He was behaving as if he was out of his _____.
4 The previous chapters will already have given you plenty of food for _____.
5 Off the top of your _____, what do you know about Vitamin C?
6 Rack your _____ and tell me everything you now about him.

Exercise 2

Decide if the following sentences are true (*T*) or false (*F*).

1 If something crosses your mind, you forget about it. ☐
2 If something rings a bell, it reminds you of something. ☐
3 If you have a gut reaction to something, you have spent a long time thinking about it. ☐
4 If you say something off the top of your head, you are very strange and dangerous. ☐
5 If something is food for thought, it makes you think. ☐
6 If you are racking your brain, you aren't thinking very hard. ☐

Exercise 3

Choose the best answer to complete the sentences.

1 'Do you know anyone called Frascati?' – 'Well the name _____.'

   a racks my brains   b rings a bell   c is miles away

2 'Dr Barth, what is the greatest single thought that ever _____?'

   a rang a bell   b racked your brains   c crossed your mind

3 'You don't know anyone else who might be free?' – 'Not _____, no.'

   a on the tip of my tongue b crossing my mind   c off the top of my head

4 I'm just trying to remember his name; it's _____.

   a racking my brains   b on the tip of my tongue c crossing my mind

5 'Did you ask me a question? I'm sorry, I was _____!'

   a miles away   b out of my mind   c ringing a bell

6 Someone mentioned this point recently and I'm _____ to think who it was.

   a out of my mind   b racking my brains   c bearing it in mind

Exercise 4

Correct the idioms in these sentences.

1 Business has been very bad and the management seem to have racked the plot.
2 You can withdraw money at other banks but bear in thought that they might charge a handling fee.
3 You are off your mind if you think I'll help you commit a crime!
4 Off the top of his mind, he couldn't think of an excuse she would believe.
5 The after-dinner speaker provided us with plenty of thought food.
6 Her name was on the top of my tongue, but I just couldn't get it.
7 Personally, I trust my gut action to tell me when I'm right.
8 It crossed my head that I hadn't heard the children for a while.

Exercise 5

Choose the most appropriate thing A–H to say in each situation 1–8.

1 Someone gives you a useful tip for your next trip abroad.

2 You're telling someone about a thought-provoking talk you've just heard.

3 A friend has just told you about an extreme sport he wants to try and you think it's too dangerous.

4 You're trying hard to remember the answer to a quiz question.

5 A friend has mentioned someone's name and asked you if you know that person. You aren't sure but the name sounds familiar.

6 You realize that you haven't been listening to something a friend has been telling you, because you were thinking about something else.

7 You have to explain why you burst out laughing when you saw your photo in the paper.

8 Someone asks you if you have ever thought about working abroad.

A It has crossed my mind.

B You're out of your mind!

C It's on the tip of my tongue.

D The name rings a bell.

E Sorry, I was miles away.

F It's certainly given me food for thought.

G Thanks, I'll keep it in mind.

H It was just a gut reaction.

Exercise 6

Complete the table with idioms from this unit.

remembering and forgetting	1 _____
	2 _____
	3 _____
	4 _____
	5 _____
thinking	1 _____
	2 _____
	3 _____
	4 _____
not thinking logically	1 _____
	2 _____
	3 _____
	4 _____

Your turn!

Have you had trouble remembering something in the last few days? Use the idioms from this unit to describe your experience. For example:

I couldn't remember the Italian word for butterfly yesterday although it was on the tip of my tongue.

Sometimes I have a mind like a sieve and by the afternoon, I can't recall anything from my morning lessons.

Fortunately, she knew he had **a mind like a sieve.**

Communicating

at cross purposes

If two people are at cross purposes, they think they are talking about or trying to do the same thing as each other, but they are actually talking about or trying to do different things.

They had been talking at cross purposes earlier, he realized. They hadn't been offering him a share of the deal at all.

come out of your shell

If you come out of your shell, you become less shy and more confident.

NOTE   The image here is of a snail or shellfish, both of which go into their shells for protection.

She used to be very timid and shy but I think she's come out of her shell.

NOTE   You can say that someone or something brings you out of your shell when they cause you to be less shy and more confident.

I think the job has brought her out of her shell.

find common ground

If two people or groups who generally disagree find common ground, they find a particular subject or opinion that they agree about.

Both leaders were keen to stress that they were seeking to find common ground.

from the horse's mouth

If you get a piece of information from the horse's mouth, you get it directly from someone who is involved in it and knows the most about it.

NOTE   This expression may refer to the fact that you can tell a horse's age by looking at its teeth.

When he tells them, straight from the horse's mouth, what a good assistant you are, they'll increase your wages.

get your wires crossed or get your lines crossed

If you get your wires crossed or get your lines crossed, you are mistaken about what someone else means.

NOTE   People used to say they had a crossed line when their phone call was connected wrongly and they could hear someone else's conversation.

She looked confused at what he said and he began to wonder if he'd got his wires crossed.

He'd got his lines crossed: 'What part of America are you from?' he asked. 'Sweden,' came the reply.

go off on a tangent or go off at a tangent

If a person or piece of writing goes off on a tangent or goes off at a tangent, they start saying or thinking something that is not directly connected with what they were saying or thinking before.

NOTE   In geometry, a tangent is a straight line which touches a curve at one point.

Our teacher would occasionally go off on a tangent and start talking about something totally unrelated to the textbook.

NOTE   You can use other verbs instead of go.

The book's theme wanders off on a tangent now and then.

hear something through the grapevine or hear something on the grapevine

If you hear something through the grapevine or hear something on the grapevine, you are told a piece of news informally by someone who was told it by someone else.

NOTE   One of the early telegraph systems in America was given the nickname 'the grapevine telegraph' because the wires often became tangled, so that they reminded people of grapevines.

I heard through the grapevine that she was looking for work.

She heard on the grapevine that he had come back to London.

in black and white

If you say that something is in black and white, you mean that you have written proof of it.

We have a strict, clear rule in black and white, that this sort of behaviour will not be tolerated.

in the loop

If someone is in the loop, they are part of a group of people who have information about a particular thing.

Not many people knew what was going on but the president was almost certainly in the loop.

keep someone posted

If you keep someone posted, you continue giving them the latest information about a situation.

She made me promise to keep her posted on developments here while she was in London.

let the cat out of the bag

If you let the cat out of the bag, you reveal something secret or private, often without meaning to.

NOTE   Perhaps from an old trick where a person pretended to sell a piglet in a bag, although the bag really contained a cat. If the cat was let out of the bag, then the trick would be exposed.

'They didn't tell the cops my name, did they?' 'Of course not,' she said. 'They wouldn't want to let the cat out of the bag.'

put someone in the picture

If you put someone in the picture, you tell them about a situation that they need to know about.

I believe that I could now produce evidence to prove my case, so let me put you in the picture.

spill the beans

If you spill the beans, you reveal the truth about something secret or private. [INFORMAL]

NOTE   This expression has a number of possible explanations. One refers to an ancient way of voting by placing coloured beans in jars or pots, then tipping the beans out and counting them.

He was scared to death I was going to spill the beans to the cops.

touch base

If you touch base with someone, you contact them, often when you have not spoken to them or seen them for a long time.

NOTE   In baseball, batters have to touch the first, second, and third bases to score a run.

A brief phone-call is often made to touch base and update the parent on any developments.

Exercise 1

Match phrases 1–8 with A–H to make idioms from this unit.

1 go off at
2 get your wires
3 to be
4 keep someone
5 spill
6 touch
7 let the cat out of
8 put someone in

A the bag
B base
C a tangent
D the beans
E the picture
F posted
G at cross purposes
H crossed

Exercise 2

Complete the sentences with the words in the box. Some of the sentences have more than one answer.

| out | from | at | in | off | on |

1 Keep me _____ the loop, will you?
2 I wish she wouldn't keep going off _____ a tangent.
3 We heard a rumour _____ the grapevine.
4 Let me put you _____ the picture.
5 I heard all this straight _____ the horse's mouth.
6 I think they were arguing _____ cross purposes there.
7 She promised me she wouldn't let the cat _____ of the bag.
8 She really came _____ of her shell when the singing started.

Exercise 3

Re-order the phrases to make sentences. Add punctuation where necessary.

1 true / it must be / here in black and white / because it's
2 as you develop / keep me / the idea / in the loop
3 every week to / touch base / we meet / have lunch and
4 was moving / that the discussion /off on a tangent / I thought
5 she was doing / she asked him / on how / to keep her posted
6 paid / the office cleaner to / the newspaper reporter / spill the beans
7 the issue of / find common ground on / they managed to / rates of pay
8 going away / the family agreed that / would bring him out of his shell / to university

Exercise 4

Make sentences 1–6 less formal. Replace the <u>underlined</u> words with the correct idioms A–F.

1 I haven't heard any news yet, but I'll <u>inform you</u>.
2 It was meant to be a surprise, but someone <u>gave the secret away</u>.
3 I <u>heard a rumour</u> that Penny and Alan are getting married.
4 It must be true. I <u>heard it from a reliable source</u>.
5 Let's meet up next week just to <u>make contact again</u>.
6 They support different teams but they <u>agreed with each other</u> when someone mentioned the off-side rule.

A let the cat out of the bag
B heard on the grapevine
C keep you posted
D found common ground
E heard it straight from the horse's mouth
F touch base

Exercise 5

Match idioms 1–6 with situations A–F.

1 Jo and Dee learnt that Bud was being fired when Baz told them what he'd heard from Amit.

2 First the professor was talking about dinosaurs, then somehow it was the price of oranges!

3 This diamond was found by a workman on a building site. He told me about it himself.

4 I think we should tell Lee that the time of the meeting has been changed.

5 I thought we were going to the cinema and he thought I was cooking him dinner!

6 Nobody knew about the baby until Suzi mentioned maternity leave.

A We got our wires crossed.

B I got it from the horse's mouth.

C She let the cat out of the bag.

D They heard it on the grapevine.

E Let's put him in the picture.

F He went off at a tangent.

Exercise 6

Complete the table. Put the idioms in the correct groups.

keep someone in the picture	go off at/on a tangent	hear something on the grapevine
keep someone posted	let the cat out of the bag	get your wires crossed	in the loop
touch base	from the horse's mouth	at cross purposes	spill the beans	in black and white

communicating badly	1 _____
	2 _____
	3 _____
maintaining communication	1 _____
	2 _____
	3 _____
	4 _____
revealing a secret	1 _____
	2 _____
trusting information	1 _____
	2 _____
	3 _____

Your turn!

Think about the way you've communicated with people around you recently. Use the idioms from this unit to describe a situation from the last few days. For example:

My teacher went off on a tangent and started telling us about her holiday.

I heard on the grapevine that Petra's getting married.

Sometimes, even your friends **let the cat out of the bag.**

4

Priorities and decisions

the bottom line

In a discussion or argument, the bottom line is the most important and basic fact about what you are discussing.

NOTE A reference to the last line in a set of accounts, which states how much money has been made.

*The bottom line **is that the great majority of our kids are physically unfit.***

cross that bridge when you come to it

If you say 'I'll cross that bridge when I come to it', you mean that you will deal with a problem when, or if, it happens.

'You can't make me talk to you'. 'No, but the police can'. 'I'll cross that bridge when I come to it'.

cut to the chase

If you cut to the chase, you start talking about or dealing with what is really important, instead of less important things.

NOTE In films, when one scene ends and another begins the action is said to 'cut' from one scene to the next. If a film 'cuts to the chase', it moves on to a car chase scene, which is usually fast-moving and exciting.

*I'll cut to the chase – **we just don't have enough money for the project.***

the icing on the cake

If you describe something as the icing on the cake, you mean that it is an extra good thing that makes a good situation or activity even better.

To play for one's country is the ultimate experience. To be in a winning team is the icing on the cake.

in two minds

If you are in two minds about something, you are not able to reach a decision or opinion about something.

*Roche was in two minds **whether to make the trip to Oslo.***

make a mountain out of a molehill

If someone makes a mountain out of a molehill, they talk or complain about a small, unimportant problem as if it is important and serious.

*Don't make a mountain out of a molehill – **it's really not a big deal.***

on the back burner

If you put a project or issue on the back burner, you decide not to do anything about it until a later date.

*People's dreams have once again been put on the back burner **as they concern themselves with surviving from one day to the next.***

NOTE Different prepositions allow you to use the back burner in other ways with a similar meaning.

Healthcare workers worry that the expense will push this issue onto a back burner.

In this climate, website development is an obvious candidate for the back burner.

play it by ear

If you play it by ear, you deal with things as they happen, rather than following a plan or previous arrangement.

NOTE   If someone plays a piece of music by ear, they play it without looking at printed music.

'Where will we stay in Gloucestershire?' 'Oh, I'm not sure yet. We'll have to play it by ear'.

sit on the fence

If you sit on the fence, you refuse to give a definite opinion about something or to say who you support in an argument.

NOTE   The fence referred to is one that separates two properties or territories and someone sitting on it is unable or unwilling to make a decision about which side to stand on.

Which do you prefer: chocolate or vanilla ice-cream? You can't sit on the fence and say you like both of them equally.

NOTE   Verbs such as stay and be can be used instead of sit.

Democrats who'd been on the fence about the nomination, in the end all voted for him.

split hairs

If someone splits hairs, they argue about very small details or find very small differences between things which are really very similar.

Many of the cases the reporter mentioned were not, in fact, on the original list, but let's not split hairs.

stick to your guns

If you stick to your guns, you refuse to change your decision or opinion about something, even though other people are trying to tell you that you are wrong.

NOTE   Think of soldiers remaining in position, even though they are being attacked by the enemy.

Once you have decided what is and isn't acceptable, stick to your guns despite your child's protests.

take a back seat

If you take a back seat, you allow other people to have all the power, importance, or responsibility.

I was happy to take a back seat and give someone else the opportunity to manage the project.

the tip of the iceberg

If something is the tip of the iceberg, it is a small part of a very large problem or a very serious situation.

NOTE   Only about one tenth of an iceberg is visible above the water. Most of it is below the surface.

We get about 2,000 complaints every year and that's just the tip of the iceberg.

up in the air

If an important decision or plan is up in the air, it has not been decided or arranged yet. *At the moment, the fate of the Hungarian people is still up in the air.*

Exercise 1

Complete the sentences with the words in the box.

| by | of | to | in | on |

1 We're just going to play it _____ ear.
2 This is just the tip _____ the iceberg.
3 Let's put that decision _____ the back burner for now.
4 I'm _____ two minds about spending all that money at once.
5 He stuck _____ his guns in spite of their grumbling.
6 We'll cross that bridge when we come _____ it.

Exercise 2

Match sentence halves 1–6 with A–F to make complete sentences.

1 The bottom line is simply
2 We're going to play it by ear
3 You will have to stop sitting on the fence
4 The answer should have a capital letter
5 Let's skip the introductions
6 We can't ignore this issue

A and cut straight to the chase.
B but let's not make a mountain out of a molehill.
C but I won't split hairs.
D and see how the next 24 hours go.
E that business is about money.
F and show where your loyalty lies.

Exercise 3

Choose the best answer to complete the sentences.

1 'They really believe in what I do and they want to enable me to do it.' She went on to explain her success: 'I'm very good, that's _____.'

   a the bottom line   b the tip of the iceberg   c the back burner

2 Then he became really ill and had to put all his plans _____.

   a up in the air   b on the fence   c on the back burner

3 'What if you need another operation after this one?' – 'I'll _____.'

   a make a mountain out of a molehill   b cross that bridge when I come to it

   c stick to my guns

4 The President accused his critics of being oversensitive and of _____.

   a playing it by ear   b cutting to the chase   c making a mountain out of a molehill

5 For four hours of questioning, Grommek _____, but by five o'clock he had changed his story.

   a played it by ear   b cut to the chase   c stuck to his guns

6 She was _____ about whether or not to turn back.

   a splitting hairs   b in two minds   c up in the air

Exercise 4

Correct the idioms in these sentences.

1 The dates for the summit meeting are still up on the fence at the moment.
2 The police say that these numbers could just be the top of the iceberg.
3 He'll do what he can to make you change your mind, but you stick on the back burner.
4 I'd don't want to retire when I'm sixty years old but I'll cut to the bridge when I come to it.
5 She forgot her notes so she had to play it by air at the interview.
6 There just isn't any more money and that sits on the bottom line.
7 After he retires, Ken will be able to sit in the back seat in the family business.
8 I was proud to work for Ferrari, and to drive their fantastic cars was the icing in the cake.

Exercise 5

Complete the sentences with idioms in this unit, changing the verb forms if necessary.

1 I was so pleased just to have passed the exam; coming first was _____.
2 I can't really say too much about who else I'm going to be working with at the moment because it's all very much _____ and anything could happen.
3 I never really had a plan for my life. I just _____. Neither of us is very ambitious and we have enough money.
4 She introduced herself and then said 'I'll _____: I have all the evidence I need to put you in prison for the next ten years'.
5 This is a misleading figure. There will be many hidden costs that we will discover as this project develops. I suggest that £1.4 billion is only _____.
6 Yet on this key issue, the government has chosen to _____, saying that schools must decide for themselves.
7 He warned reporters not to _____. 'I'm disappointed, but it's not heartbreaking', he said. 'It was far worse in 1996.'
8 I'm fed up with being the boss so I'm going to _____ and let other people do the hard work for a while.

Exercise 6

Complete the table with idioms from this unit.

emphasizing something important	1 _____
	2 _____
showing that something is less important	1 _____
	2 _____
	3 _____
	4 _____
a decision not yet made	1 _____
	2 _____
	3 _____
	4 _____

Your turn!

Have you had to decide how important something is in your life recently? Use the idioms in this unit to talk about it. For example:

I stuck to my guns *told my parents I wanted to go travelling.*

I don't know what I'll do after my exams – I'll cross that bridge when I come to it.

The nurse thought Jim was making a mountain out of a molehill.

5

Relationships

break the ice

If a person, event or activity breaks the ice, they make people feel more relaxed and comfortable in a social situation.

NOTE   This refers to the need to break the ice around a ship before it is able to sail.

This exercise is usually good fun and can help break the ice for a new, and perhaps rather anxious, group.

NOTE   An ice-breaker is something that you say or do to break the ice.

This presentation, with a few additional jokes, was a good ice-breaker.

get off on the wrong foot

If you get off on the wrong foot, you start a relationship or an activity badly.

NOTE   The 'wrong foot' refers to the left foot. There is an ancient superstition that the left side of the body is connected with bad luck and evil.

We got off on the wrong foot the first time I met him, but that's all forgotten now.

NOTE   You can also say start off on the wrong foot.

Their relationship had started off on the wrong foot.

get on like a house on fire

If two people get on like a house on fire, they quickly become close friends.

NOTE   This expression uses the image of an old wooden house burning suddenly and strongly.

I went over and struck up a conversation, and we got on like a house on fire.

get on someone's nerves

If someone or something gets on your nerves, they irritate you.

She talks all the time and it gets on my nerves.

give someone the cold shoulder

If someone gives you the cold shoulder, they deliberately stop being friendly to you and ignore you.

NOTE   In the Middle Ages, important guests were given roast meat. Less important people were only given cold meat – perhaps a shoulder – left over from previous meals.

He was upset to find his previously friendly colleagues giving him the cold shoulder.

NOTE   You can also say that you get the cold shoulder from someone.

Nancy found she was getting the cold shoulder from a lot of people she'd thought were her friends.

go back a long way

If two or more people go back a long way, they have been friends for a very long time. [mainly BRITISH]

We go back a long way, and she's always kept in touch, always been there for me.

hit it off

If two people hit it off when they first meet, they like each other and get on well together.

I had to leave because my manager was awful. We never really hit it off.

leave someone in the lurch

If someone leaves you in the lurch, they put you in a difficult situation by suddenly going away or stopping helping you.

NOTE 'The lurch' is a position of disadvantage in a card game called cribbage.

My secretary left me in the lurch last month and I haven't found a replacement yet.

on the rocks

If a relationship is on the rocks, it is experiencing many difficulties and is likely to end.

NOTE The image here is of a ship that is stuck on some rocks. *It's rumoured that their ten-year relationship is on the rocks.*

on the same wavelength

If two people are on the same wavelength, they understand each other well because they share the same attitudes, interests, and opinions.

NOTE You cannot hear a radio broadcast unless you tune to the correct wavelength.

Wendy's sister is ten years older than her, and the two are not close. 'We've never really been on the same wavelength' said Wendy.

save face

If you save face, you do something so that people continue to respect you and your reputation is not damaged.

NOTE This comes from a Chinese expression which refers to keeping a calm expression and managing to avoid the disgrace of showing one's emotions.

Most children have a need to save face in front of their friends.

sparks fly

If sparks fly between two people, they get angry with each other and argue.

The group leader is not afraid to raise difficult issues or let the sparks fly when necessary.

treat someone like dirt

If a person treats someone like dirt, they treat them very badly.

As long as unemployment is rising, the bosses can keep treating you like dirt.

your own flesh and blood

If someone is your own flesh and blood, they are a member of your family.

You can't just let your own flesh and blood go to prison if there's any way you can help.

Exercise 1

Look at the sentences below. Which three idioms have the same meaning? Which idiom has the opposite meaning to these three?

A Everyone around the table remained silent and I tried to think of a way of breaking the ice.

B It's strange that her two ex-husbands get on like a house on fire!

C Oh yes, we go back a long way – we went to nursery school together.

D I'm afraid we got off on the wrong foot because I got her name wrong.

E They are definitely on the same wavelength – both passionate about green politics.

F We didn't really hit it off – we just aren't interested in the same things.

Exercise 2

Match sentence halves 1–8 with A–H to make complete sentences.

1	Whenever his mother was in the room,	A	definitely on the rocks.
2	It's his stupid loud voice	B	I was aware of sparks flying.
3	Their business partnership was now	C	treated them like dirt.
4	She took his keys and his coat	D	our own flesh and blood.
5	They left because the manager	E	and left him in the lurch.
6	He was rude to her so she's decided that in future	F	that gets on my nerves.
7	We care about you because you are	G	to help them save face.
8	We pretended not to notice them leave,	H	she'll give him the cold shoulder.

Exercise 3

Choose the best answer to complete the sentences.

1 You have started _____ by arriving late for our appointment.

    a to save face   b on the same wavelength   c off on the wrong foot

2 He's highly educated and she's got no qualifications at all, but they managed to _____.

    a get off on the wrong foot   b hit it off   c go back a long way

3 Mr Sen invited them all to dinner at his house to _____.

    a get off on the wrong foot   b get on like a house on fire   c break the ice

4 As soon as the prisoners arrive, the guards begin to _____.

    a treat them like dirt   b get off on the wrong foot   c leave them in the lurch

5 Luca's personal assistant quit suddenly and _____ so I'm doing some typing for him.

    a left him in the lurch   b treated him like dirt   c got the cold shoulder

6 They argue all the time now. There's no doubt that their marriage is _____.

    a on fire   b on the rocks   c their own flesh and blood

Exercise 4

Correct the idioms in these sentences.

1 When I saw her at the party, she just gave me the cold hands.

2 We used to argue a lot, but now we're getting on like a house in the lurch.

3 We go back on the rocks. We met when we were just children.

4 As soon as they met, they hit it on.

5 I find him a bit irritating. He really gets on my sparks.

6 We understand each other well. We're on the same foot.

Exercise 5

Replace the underlined words with idioms from this unit in the correct form.

1 We get on well, but we have different views on politics. As soon as we start talking about politics, <u>we have an argument</u> – so we tend to avoid the subject.

2 Don't worry – I promised I would help you, and I won't <u>abandon you</u>.

3 Unfortunately when we first met, we <u>had a disagreement which ruined our relationship</u>. But I'm sure that next time we meet, we can become friends.

4 I tried to say something funny just to <u>ease the tension</u> – but I don't think she found it very amusing.

5 Jenny and your brother seem to <u>have enjoyed each other's company right from the start</u> – they've been talking together for ages.

6 I think he should resign. His boss <u>shows no respect for him</u> and he deserves better.

7 Most of the time I was terrified, but trying to <u>appear unaffected</u>, I did my best to stay cool.

8 I was shocked to hear her speaking to <u>a member of her family</u> like that.

Exercise 6

Complete the table. Put the idioms in the correct groups.

treat someone like dirt | go back a long way | get off on the wrong foot | sparks fly
give someone the cold shoulder | get on like a house on fire | get on someone's nerves
hit it off | on the same wavelength | leave someone in the lurch | on the rocks

successful relationships	1 _____
	2 _____
	3 _____
	4 _____
bad relationships	1 _____
	2 _____
	3 _____
	4 _____
	5 _____
	6 _____
	7 _____

Your turn!

Use the idioms in this unit to describe your relationships with friends, classmates, colleagues and family. For example:

Ramesh and I go back a long way – we went to school together.

My sister left me in the lurch when she borrowed my last £5 and didn't pay it back.

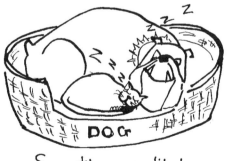

Sometimes unlikely friends can get on like a house on fire.

6

Help and encouragement

bend over backwards or bend over backward

If you bend over backwards or bend over backward, you try very hard to help or please someone, even though it causes you trouble.

We bent over backwards to make them feel welcome and they didn't thank us once.

be there for someone

If you are there for someone, you are ready to listen to their problems and to help and support them. [SPOKEN]

Jimmy is a good friend – he's always been there for me when I needed help or advice.

give and take

If you talk about give and take, you mean the way in which two people or groups in a relationship accept that they cannot have everything that they want and that they must sometimes give the other person or group what they want.

All good partnerships involve a bit of give and take.

hold someone's hand

If you hold someone's hand in an unfamiliar or difficult situation, you help and support them.

Tony will hold your hand through the sale, deal with offers and advise on any problems.

in the same boat

If two or more people are in the same boat, they are in the same unpleasant or difficult situation.

Don't worry if you are going bald – 40 per cent of men under 35 are in the same boat.

keep your chin up

If you keep your chin up, you stay cheerful in a difficult or unpleasant situation.

Richards was keeping his chin up yesterday despite the continued setbacks.

lend a hand or lend someone a hand

If you lend a hand or lend someone a hand, you help someone to do something.

If I'd known you were having trouble, I could have lent a hand.

Could you lend me a hand with these books, please?

NOTE   A hand is used in many other structures with a similar meaning.

I used to give Mary a hand with the catering

Need a hand with those?

Do you want a hand with the children?

look the other way

If someone looks the other way, they deliberately ignore something bad that is happening when they should be trying to deal with it or stop it.

NOTE   You usually use this expression to suggest that this is a bad thing to do.

The government is fully aware of the problem but they just look the other way.

meet someone halfway

If you meet someone halfway, you accept some of their opinions or wishes, so that you can come to an agreement with them or have a better relationship with them.

The opposition is willing to meet the president halfway on his latest plans for the economy.

a pat on the back

If you give someone a pat on the back, you praise them for something they have done.

The industry can give itself a little pat on the back for the positive moves it has made to help its own recovery.

NOTE   You can also say pat someone on the back, or pat yourself on the back.

I thought the editor would pat me on the back and say, 'Well done!' Instead he fired me.

Today is a good day to pat yourself on the back for bravery and effort.

put your heads together

If people put their heads together, they try to solve a problem together.

If there's a problem, we all just sit down, put our heads together and figure it out.

sing someone's praises

If you sing someone's or something's praises, you praise them in an enthusiastic way.

Smith continued to sing Tony's praises. 'He's so different, he's so natural', he said.

take someone under your wing

If you take someone under your wing, you start to look after them and make sure that they are well and have what they need.

NOTE   The image here is of a hen gathering her chicks under her wing.

She took the youngster under her wing, gave her advice and helped her prepare for the tour.

a tower of strength or a pillar of strength

If someone is a tower of strength or a pillar of strength during a difficult period in your life, they give you a lot of help or support.

My eldest daughter was a tower of strength for me when I was sick.

In her terrible sadness she has found Charles to be a pillar of strength.

Exercise 1

Complete the sentences with the words in the box.

| over | up | together | in | on | under |

1 I phoned to give you a pat _____ the back for saving the situation.
2 Let's put our heads _____ and think of some people who could help.
3 As we're both _____ the same boat, it might be sensible to work together.
4 Most parents bend _____ backwards to treat their children equally.
5 Jane took us _____ her wing and showed us around.
6 I try to think positively and keep my chin _____.

Exercise 2

Choose the best answer to complete the sentences.

1 There is usually a fair amount of _____ and take in a trading relationship.

   a pat   b give   c hand

2 They want to negotiate and we're very willing to _____ them halfway.

   a meet   b bend   c hold

3 Hannah was happy to _____ a hand in practical ways if she could.

   a pat   b lend   c take

4 For most of the afternoon, Mum had been _____ Cyril's praises.

   a giving   b putting   c singing

5 I want to be _____ for my kids because my dad wasn't for me.

   a there   b together   c over

6 The government finds it easiest to _____ the other way regarding this issue.

   a look   b bend   c keep

Exercise 3

Answer the questions.

1 If you take someone under your wing, do you ignore or help them?
2 If you keep your chin up, are you being cheerful or miserable?
3 If you give someone a pat on the back, should they be pleased or offended?
4 If you bend over backwards, are you ignoring someone or trying to help them?
5 If someone lends you a hand, are you being helpful, or are they being helpful to you?
6 If you hold someone's hand in a difficult situation, do you need help or do you give help?

Exercise 4

Re-order the phrases to make sentences. Add punctuation where necessary.

1 women candidates / bends over backwards / to attract / the party
2 learn that / girls and boys / give and take / there must be / in all relationships
3 lend a hand with / the whole family / the harvest / has to
4 they must / sensible decision / in order to reach a / put their heads together
5 for you / you know / be there / I'll always
6 choose to / what should we / look the other way / do if our elected representatives

Exercise 5

Match idioms 1–8 with definitions A–H.

1 Keep your chin up. I'm sure everything will be alright in the end.

2 If we put our heads together, we'll come up with a solution.

3 You must have made a good impression on the manager – he was singing your praises!

4 The trouble is, so many of us look the other way when we realize there's a problem.

5 I know how you feel. I'm in the same boat as you.

6 His parents bend over backwards for him but they get no thanks.

7 I'll do what I can for him just now but I can't hold his hand forever.

8 My husband has been a tower of strength throughout this ordeal.

A do everything possible to help

B in an identical situation

C stay optimistic

D support him

E being complimentary about you

F deliberately ignore the situation

G someone who is helpful and supportive

H work as a team

Exercise 6

Use sentences A–H to answer questions 1–8.

1 Who was a kind and supportive mother?

2 Who likes to find a compromise?

3 Who was given a generous welcome?

4 Who found someone to help him?

5 Who is rather pleased with what he has done?

6 Who was a kind and supportive father?

7 Who is managing to remain cheerful?

8 Who thinks that other people have similar problems?

A Rakesh gave himself a pat on the back for finishing early.

B Smith and Burnet's policy with customers who complain is to try to meet them halfway.

C Mr Chang took Ewen under his wing and treated him like a son.

D Lisa told herself there were plenty of girls in the same boat as her.

E Sven returned from New York singing the praises of American hospitality.

F Sasha hasn't found a job yet, but she's keeping her chin up.

G Maria was a pillar of strength when her children had so many problems.

H Manuelle held his son's hand throughout his marriage break-up.

Your turn!

Use the idioms in this unit to describe how someone has helped or encouraged you, or how you have helped someone else. For example:

I'm finding the grammar classes really difficult but it helps to know we're all in the same boat.

My colleagues and I put our heads together and submitted the winning proposal.

The chickens were **in the same boat.**

Involvement and interest

not be your cup of tea

If something is not your cup of tea, you do feel very interested or enthusiastic about it.

I've never been the greatest traveller. Sitting for hours on motorways is not really my cup of tea.

NOTE   You can also say that something or someone is your cup of tea when you like them or feel interested in them.

I don't have much time for modern literature. Shakespeare's more my cup of tea.

have an axe to grind

If someone has an axe to grind, they have particular attitudes about something, often because they think they have been treated badly or because they want to get an advantage.

NOTE   One possible explanation for this expression is a story told by the American scientist and inventor Benjamin Franklin (1706–90) about a man who managed to get his own axe sharpened without paying by asking a boy to show him how his father's grindstone (=a round stone used for sharpening metal tools or weapons) worked.

It would be best if an independent agency, that doesn't have an axe to grind, could deal with this case.

NOTE   You can also say that you have no axe to grind to deny that your strong opinions about something are based on personal reasons.

The unions insist they have no axe to grind, because they will represent workers wherever they are based.

in the picture

If someone is in the picture, they are involved in the situation you are talking about.

We were a great team. I was kept in the picture from the beginning.

jump on the bandwagon

If someone jumps on the bandwagon, they suddenly become involved in an activity because it is likely to succeed or it is fashionable.

NOTE   In American elections in the past, political rallies (=large public meetings) often included a band playing on a horse-drawn wagon (=a covered vehicle pulled by horses). Politicians sat on the wagon and those who wanted to show their support climbed on it.

There will always be people ready to jump on the bandwagon and start classes in whatever is fashionable, with little or no training.

NOTE   Verbs such as climb, get and leap are sometimes used instead of jump. These expressions are usually used in a disapproving way.

A lot of people are climbing on the bandwagon of selling financial services to women.

keep a low profile

If someone keeps a low profile, they avoid doing things that will make people notice them.

The president continues to keep a low profile on vacation in Maine.

NOTE   You can also use low-profile before a noun.

There is no need for the presence of any police officers. This is a low-profile event.

a labour of love

A labour of love is a task that you do because you enjoy it or feel strongly that it is worth doing.

They restored the Victorian greenhouse, an expensive labour of love.

mean business

If you mean business, you are serious and determined about what you are doing.

One of them pointed a shotgun at me. I could see he meant business.

a nosey parker

A nosey parker is someone who wants to know too much about other people. [BRITISH, INFORMAL]

NOTE   'Parker' may refer to Matthew Parker, who was an English archbishop in the sixteenth century and had a reputation for interfering in people's business.

The village's nosey parker, Olive, likes to spy on her neighbours with binoculars.

NOTE   'Nosey' is sometimes spelled 'nosy'.

poke your nose into something or stick your nose into something

If someone pokes or sticks their nose into something, they interfere in something that does not concern them. [INFORMAL]

He has no right to go poking his nose into my affairs.

Why did you have to go and stick your nose in?

NOTE   Keep your nose out of something means the opposite of poke your nose into something.

Nancy realized that this was his way of telling her to keep her nose out of his business.

steer clear of something

If you steer clear of someone or something, you deliberately avoid them.

I'd advise anyone with sensitive or dry skin to steer clear of soap.

try your hand at something

If you try your hand at something, you try doing it in order to see whether you are good at it.

After he left school, he tried his hand at a variety of jobs – bricklayer, baker, post man.

up to your ears

If you are up to your ears in work or in an unpleasant situation, you are very busy with it or are deeply involved in it.

I can't come out this evening – I'm up to my ears in reports.

whet someone's appetite

If something whets your appetite for a particular thing, it makes you want it.

Winning the World Championship should have whetted his appetite for more success.

NOTE   Most speakers of English only ever use the verb 'whet' in this expression. It is rarely used elsewhere.

your heart isn't in something

If your heart isn't in something you are doing, you are not enthusiastic about it.

She was a successful teacher, popular with her pupils and her colleagues, but her heart wasn't in it.

Exercise 1

Choose the best answer to complete the sentences.

1 Come to our arts and crafts evening and try your _____ at something different.

   a nose   b heart   c hand

2 Don't stick your _____ into matters that don't concern you.

   a ears   b nose   c hand

3 Everyone stayed late yesterday – we're up to our _____ in work at the office.

   a hearts   b ears   c noses

4 The rebuilding of the church organ was a real labour of _____.

   a love   b heart   c business

5 The new committee at the sports club are making lots of changes and they really mean _____!

   a heart   b labour   c business

6 We believe that the judge is fair and has no _____ to grind.

   a axe   b bandwagon   c appetite

Exercise 2

Match sentence halves 1–6 with A–F to make complete sentences.

1 It looks as though more and more companies   A wasn't in the picture at all.

2 I knew karate and had   B my heart wasn't in it.

3 I congratulated the winners but   C the ability to steer clear of danger.

4 I never wanted to be famous and I like   D will soon be leaping on the bandwagon.

5 He has decided that art history   E to keep a low profile.

6 He spoke as if I had nothing to do with it, as though I   F is not his cup of tea.

Exercise 3

Decide if the following sentences are true (T) or (F).

1 If you have an axe to grind, you have certain attitudes that are based on personal experience. ☐

2 If you jump on the bandwagon, you don't want to follow others in becoming involved in an activity. ☐

3 If you steer clear of something, you want to get involved. ☐

4 If you are up to your ears in something, you are very busy or involved. ☐

5 If someone is a nosey parker, they want to know more information than they need. ☐

6 If you keep a low profile, you want to become visibly involved in something. ☐

Exercise 4

Read the sentences and choose the best explanation.

1 His heart isn't really in it.

   a He hates it.   b He isn't completely happy with it.

2 I'm going to try my hand at pottery.

   a I'm going to see what it's like.   b I'm not going to continue doing it.

3 It really sounds as if he means business.

   a I think he's serious about it.   b I don't think he's serious about it.

4 I made this card myself. It was a real labour of love.

   a It didn't take long   b I worked very hard at it.

5 I don't want to poke my nose into your business.

   a I respect your privacy.   b I want to be involved.

6 I'd steer clear of that issue, if I were you.

   a I'd get involved.   b I would avoid it.

Exercise 5

Replace the <u>underlined</u> words with the correct idioms in the box.

> really my cup of tea | up to my ears | jump on the bandwagon | steer clear of | mean business
> have an axe to grind

Pat: Hi, George. How are you?

George: Hi, Pat. I've been [1]<u>very busy</u> for the last few months. We've taken on a lot of new clients. One of our main competitors, has been expanding rapidly. It's clear that they [2]<u>are really serious about succeeding</u>. So my boss has decided to [3]<u>follow the trend</u> and start expanding too. I don't [4]<u>have a problem</u> about the extra work, but we just don't have enough staff to deal with it all.

Pat: You should ask for a promotion.

George: I would, but then they'd expect me to work even longer hours! So I'm going to [5]<u>avoid</u> that. Anyway, I've been thinking about a career change. I'm beginning to think that software development is [6]<u>not something I enjoy</u>.

Exercise 6

Correct the idioms in these sentences.

1 I'm going to steer a low profile and hope nobody asks me to volunteer for anything at the committee meeting.
2 You certainly look like you mean to do business with your rubber gloves and apron on!
3 I wish people wouldn't poke their sticks into my business.
4 I think I'll just jump on the picture and start my diet with the rest of you.
5 It's probably best to jump clear of the city centre during the rush hour.
6 I've decided I'm going to try my heart at DIY and redecorate my room.
7 My trip to America the previous year had whetted my nose for foreign travel.
8 It's amazing how much information a serious nosy profile can find out.

Exercise 7

Complete the sentences with idioms from this unit, changing the verb and pronoun forms if necessary.

1 Writing this book has been a great pleasure, a true _____.
2 He arrived at precisely nine o'clock, wearing workmen's boots and carrying his tool kit, so we knew he

_____.
3 She did nothing to draw attention to herself, trying to _____.
4 I always try to write the same amount about each of the political parties – I don't _____.
5 If you want people to respect you, don't _____ their private affairs.
6 In the interview with Sir Allan, I _____ any questions relating to the court case.
7 After advertising six vacancies, they are now _____ in applications forms.
8 _____ at deep sea fishing or take a course in scuba diving. Beginners welcome!

Your turn!

Use the idioms in this unit to describe your involvement or interest in things in your life. For example:

I'm keeping a low profile at college because I haven't completed my assignment.

There's a concert tonight but rock music isn't really my cup of tea.

He decided that dog walking was just **not** his cup of tea.

8

Starting and stopping

call it a day

1 If you call it a day, you decide to stop doing something you have been doing that day.

I searched for hours but I had to call it a day when it got dark.

NOTE   In the evening, people sometimes say that they are going to call it a night.

Tomorrow is going to be busy, so let's call it a night.

2 If someone calls it a day, they retire from their job.

It's no secret I want his job when he calls it a day.

call it quits

If you call it quits, you decide to stop doing something or stop being involved in something.

The nightclub stays open until the last customer is ready to call it quits.

cut your losses

If you cut your losses, you decide to stop spending time, energy, or money on an activity or situation on which you have already spent a lot without having any success.

Competition in the market was very strong, so we decided to cut our losses and close the business.

enough is enough

People say enough is enough when they think that something, usually something bad, should stop.

How much longer will we allow ourselves to be insulted before saying enough is enough?

from scratch

If you do something or start something from scratch, you create something completely new, rather than adding to something that already exists.

NOTE   In the past, the starting line for races was often a line scratched in the earth.

He would rather start again from scratch with new rules, new members, and a new electoral system.

grind to a halt

If a process or an activity grinds to a halt, it gradually becomes slower or less active until it stops.

The peace process has ground to a halt.

NOTE   This expression refers to the way metal parts, for example in an engine, rub together and make a noise when they are not oiled well enough.

hit the ground running

If you hit the ground running, you start a new activity with great energy and enthusiasm, working effectively from the beginning.

NOTE   This image here may be of soldiers landing by parachute or helicopter in a battle area and moving off quickly as soon as they reach the ground.

She's having a holiday just now and will no doubt hit the ground running with all sorts of new ideas when she gets back.

in business

If you say that you are in business, you mean that you can start doing something because you have got everything ready for it. [SPOKEN]

The new software is installed and working, right? Okay, we're in business.

knock something on the head

1 If you knock a story or idea on the head, you show that it is not true or correct. [INFORMAL, BRITISH]

It's time to knock the idea that we are not living a full life unless we are married on the head.

2 If you knock an activity on the head, you stop doing it, or decide not to do it. [INFORMAL]

We'll never be a famous band. When we stop enjoying ourselves, we'll knock it on the head.

nip something in the bud

If you nip a bad situation or bad behaviour in the bud, you stop it at an early stage.

NOTE   This expression may refer to extremely cold weather damaging a plant and stopping it flowering. Alternatively, it may refer to a gardener removing buds from a plant to prevent it flowering.

It is important to recognize jealousy as soon as possible and to nip it in the bud before it becomes a serious problem.

set the ball rolling or start the ball rolling

If you set the ball rolling or start the ball rolling, you start an activity or you do something which other people will join in with later.

I've already started the ball rolling. I've set up meetings with all sorts of people.

NOTE   You can also use verbs such as get and keep.

Once you get the ball rolling, everyone wants to be involved.

turn over a new leaf

If someone has turned over a new leaf, they have started to behave in a better way than before.

While Eddie has turned over a new leaf, his brother is still racing around in fast cars and causing trouble.

up and running

If a system, business, or plan is up and running, it has started and is functioning successfully.

The project, once it is up and running, will be very dangerous.

Exercise 1

Complete the sentences with the words in the box.

ball | day | bud | halt | head | business | leaf | ground

1 Evans set the _____ rolling with a £1 million donation to the charity.
2 The family has agreed to turn over a new _____ in their relations with each other.
3 We need someone who is fully trained so that they can hit the _____ running.
4 This is worrying – we need to knock this idea on the _____ very quickly.
5 The negotiations ground to a _____ when the foreign minister walked out.
6 When the students start getting nervous you must nip it in the _____.
7 The walking group decided to call it a _____ when the rain turned to snow.
8 If you really mean _____, you'll need to buy some better gardening tools.

Exercise 2

Match idioms 1–6 with a word or phrase A–F with the same meaning.

1 I think it's time to set the ball rolling.
2 This kind of behaviour needs to be nipped in the bud.
3 You should turn over a new leaf. You might surprise yourself.
4 Is the green light flashing? Then we're in business.
5 'Enough is enough!' said the children's exasperated mother.
6 Sometimes it's quicker just to do the whole job from scratch.

A from the beginning
B off to a good start
C stopped quickly
D start
E behave better
F it's time to stop

Exercise 3

Complete the sentences. Choose the best answers.

1 The traffic was so bad that our car *ground to a halt* / *nipped it in the bud* / *cut our losses*.
2 After ten hours' studying, I decided to *hit the ground running* / *set the ball rolling* / *call it a day*.
3 Henry's a changed person. He must have *called it quits* / *been in business* / *turned over a new leaf*.
4 This situation has gone on too long. I think it's time we *knocked it on the head* / *hit the ground running* / *ground to a halt*.
5 We need someone who can start the job immediately and *nip it in the bud* / *hit the ground running* / *call it quits*.
6 I forgot to save the file, and I've lost all the work I did today. I've got to *turn over a new leaf* / *start in business* / *start from scratch*.

Exercise 4

Match idioms 1–6 with situations A–F.

1 Bob has decided to retire as manager.
2 Many of these students have never studied English before.
3 The team were amazing when they came back for the second half and won the match easily.
4 The series was getting boring so the producers decided to end it.
5 We unpacked the new PC and installed the software.
6 You should accept your failures and concentrate on your successes.

A They hit the ground running.
B They have to start from scratch.
C He is going to call it a day.
D You must cut your losses.
E They knocked it on the head.
F We got it up and running.

Exercise 5

Correct the idioms in these sentences.

1 I was exhausted, ready to call it the day, go home and fall asleep.
2 If you want a lift to the city centre, you're starting in business because that's exactly where I'm going.
3 The existing software was no longer usable and had to be rewritten from the scratch.
4 There came a point when I had to say enough is quits and the discussion had to stop.
5 Shall I stay and finish my degree or cut my loss and go travelling?
6 I'll make films for one more year and then I'm going to keep it quits.
7 The first stage of our advertising campaign is now up and turning.
8 The best way to stop an argument is to hit it in the bud.

Exercise 6

Choose the most appropriate thing to say A–F in each situation 1–6.

1 You've been working long hours. You think it's time to go home.
2 You've noticed a lot of negative behaviour in your workplace lately. You don't want it to continue.
3 You want to start an activity that you hope everyone will join in with.
4 Your new business has started and is functioning successfully.
5 Development on something is slowing down will soon stop completely.
6 You want to create something completely new, rather than improve what you already have.

A We're up and running.
B We need to nip this in the bud.

C Let's start from scratch.
D It's grinding to a halt.
E I'm going to call it day.
F I'll start the ball rolling.

Exercise 7

Complete the table with idioms from this unit.

Starting	1 _____
	2 _____
	3 _____
	4 _____
	5 _____
Stopping	1 _____
	2 _____
	3 _____
	4 _____
	5 _____
	6 _____
	7 _____
	8 _____
Both	1 _____

Your turn!

Think about something you've done recently. Use the idioms in this unit to describe the way you or another person started or stopped doing things. For example:

My computer crashed and I had to start my essay all over again from scratch.

I've been going to bed too late recently. But enough is enough, I need to get more sleep.

She decided it might be best to **call it a day.**

Effort

break your back

If you break your back to do something, you work extremely hard to try to do it.

These days you have to break your back to make a business work.

burn the candle at both ends

If you burn the candle at both ends, you try to do too much, regularly going to bed late and getting up early in the morning.

Frank seemed to delight in burning the candle at both ends. No matter how late he stayed out, he was up at five o'clock the next morning to study.

cut corners

If you cut corners, you save time, money, or effort by not following the correct procedure or rules for doing something.

He accused his manager of trying to save money by cutting corners on staff training.

not do things by halves

If you do not do things by halves, you always do things very well and thoroughly or in an extreme way.

Kim and Christopher Dunn are not a couple to do things by halves. When it came to furnishing their new home, they decided to completely redecorate the whole house.

NOTE   You can also say that someone does not do anything by halves.

Joe never did anything by halves. He regularly worked 12-hour days, was always in training for the next marathon and in his spare time, built his own house.

do your level best

If you do your level best to do something, you try as hard as you can to do it.

The President told American troops that he would do his level best to bring them home soon.

go all out

If you go all out, you try as hard as possible to achieve something.

If I had the choice over again, I would go all out for a degree in the sciences and specialize in teaching.

go the extra mile

If you go the extra mile, you make a special effort to do or achieve something.

I discovered that going the extra mile has always been a feature of successful people.

NOTE   This expression is variable, for example you can replace go with travel and mile with yard.

We will travel the extra mile to arrive at peace.

He will be remembered for his willingness to go the extra yard to help people.

land on your feet or fall on your feet

If someone lands on their feet or falls on their feet, they find themselves in a good situation by luck.

NOTE   This may refer to the belief that when a cat falls, it always lands on its feet without hurting itself.

Everything I want, she's got: a good marriage, a good home, nice children. While I struggle through life, she always lands on her feet.

not lift a finger or not raise a finger

If someone does not lift a finger or does not raise a finger to do something or to help someone, they do not do anything.

NOTE   This expression is used to criticize people for not doing anything.

This Chancellor refuses to lift a finger to help working men and women.

What kind of people accept his kind of behaviour without raising a finger to prevent it?

make a meal of something or make a meal out of something

If someone makes a meal of something or makes a meal out of it, they spend too much time or energy on it. [mainly BRITISH]

He's only been asked to write a brief essay but he's making such a meal of it.

pull your socks up

If someone tells you to pull your socks up, they want you to improve your behaviour or work. [BRITISH]

If he wants to continue in the job he'll have to pull his socks up.

pull your weight

If you pull your weight, you work as hard as everyone else who is involved in the same task or activity.

I felt that John wasn't pulling his weight around the house and asked him to do a bit more of the cleaning.

work your fingers to the bone

If you work your fingers to the bone, you work extremely hard.

I have washed, cooked, fetched and carried all my life. I work my fingers to the bone in this house.

work your socks off

If you work your socks off, you work extremely hard. [INFORMAL]

They worked their socks off to make the business succeed.

NOTE   You can use this expression with many other verbs, especially verbs related to performing such as dance, act and play. In each case, it means 'a lot' or 'very well'.

I danced my socks off last night.

Capper is currently playing his socks off for his team.

Exercise 1

Complete the sentences with the words in the box.

candle | socks | corners | fingers | socks | halves | finger | feet

1 Don't try to cut _____ as you'll only be making work for yourself later on.
2 He has fallen on his _____ with this new job – he'll earn a fortune.
3 Her boss told her she'd have to pull her _____ up.
4 You are burning the _____ at both ends if you only sleep for five hours a night.
5 As he never did things by _____, he was soon exhausted.
6 I do all the cleaning. She never lifts a _____ to help.
7 I work my _____ off for eleven months of the year. I deserve a month's holiday.
8 My grandmother had to work her _____ to the bone in the kitchen with no electrical appliances.

Exercise 2

Complete the sentences. Choose the best answers.

1 I _____ to answer all their questions.

  a did my level best   b worked my fingers to the bone   c pulled my weight

2 The President is determined to _____ for peace.

  a pull his socks up   b make a meal   c go the extra mile

3 We cannot afford to carry members who are not _____.

  a doing things by halves b making a meal of it   c pulling their weight

4 If you know what you really want, you should _____ to get it.

  a pull your weight   b go all out   c pull your socks up

5 She _____ in order to send her children to school.

  a cut corners   b worked her fingers to the bone   c made a meal of it

6 When you're _____ trying to start a business, it will take every minute you have.

  a breaking your back b raising a finger   c pulling your socks up

Exercise 3

Re-order the phrases to make sentences. Add punctuation where necessary.

1 for another win / to go all out / after last week's triumph / the team are ready
2 who have to / there are millions of people / just to stay alive / work their fingers to the bone
3 play our socks off if / we will / we want to beat them / have to
4 it's better not / by cutting corners / things cheaply / to try to do
5 a bit of trouble / but it looks like he'll / he had / land on his feet
6 a story like this / just love to / make a meal of / the newspapers

Exercise 4

Match idioms A–F with situations 1–6.

1 Jim is complaining about how hard it has been to keep his business going.

2 Sara's boss is explaining to her that she shouldn't try to get a job done by leaving out certain parts of the task.

3 Jill is complaining about her flat-mate, who is lazy and does no housework.

4 Edward is congratulating a friend who has just got a promotion and a new flat, in the same week.

5 A teacher is telling a student not to spend too long on a question that doesn't demand more than a few sentences as an answer.

6 The coach is persuading his team to make an enormous effort to win the game.

A Make the essential points but don't make a meal of it.

B You've really landed on your feet this time!

C I've been working my socks off for the past two years.

D We're playing well, but we need to go all out this time.

E It's no good trying to cut corners.

F She doesn't lift a finger.

Exercise 5

Use sentences A–H to answer questions 1–8.

1 Who didn't deliver his work on time?

2 Who worked hard to earn more than usual?

3 Who was really unhelpful?
4 Who doesn't get enough sleep?
5 Who spent too much time and energy on his homework?
6 Who didn't want to be late?
7 Who needs to work harder at school?

8 Who is a good hostess?

A Ellana didn't raise a finger when everyone else was tidying up.
B George decided it wasn't worth breaking his back to meet the deadline.
C Kiri's report said she must pull her socks up.
D Jean worked his socks off to save up for a holiday.
E Anton did his level best to arrive early.
F Anna will always go the extra mile to make people feel welcome.
G Kaz made a meal out of writing three sentences in English.
H Helen has been burning the candle at both ends recently.

Exercise 6

Correct the idioms in these sentences.

1 I've been breaking my fingers to get this work done on time.
2 She's really lucky, she seems to have landed on her back again.
3 There's no point in eating a meal of this issue.
4 If you aren't prepared to go the extra corner, you won't get the top grade.
5 He's so lazy. He doesn't lift a bone.
6 I'm exhausted. I've been working my weight off at the office today.
7 If everyone pulls their fingers they'll get a fair reward for what they do.
8 Jimmy admitted that he never did anything by half.

Your turn!

Think about how much effort you put into things. Use the idioms in this unit to describe anything you or any of your friends have done recently. For example:

Mercedes and I fell on our feet when we were upgraded to first class on our journey home.

I went the extra mile and ended up with a really good grade.

Eric's colleagues were not convinced he was **pulling his weight.**

10

Honesty and fairness

above board

If a situation or business is above board, it is honest and legal.

NOTE   This expression comes from card games in which players place their bets on a board or table. Actions above the table, where other players can see them, are probably fair.

Anyone who wants to inspect our books can see for themselves that we are totally above board.

not beat around the bush or not beat about the bush

If you don't beat around the bush or don't beat about the bush, you say what you want to say clearly and directly.

NOTE   In organized hunting, someone will drive birds or small animals out of the undergrowth by beating it with a stick. They may have to do this cautiously as they do not know exactly where the birds or animals are.

Let's not beat about the bush. I think these letters are worth a lot to you.

below the belt

If someone says something that is below the belt, they say something cruel and unfair.

NOTE   In boxing, it is against the rules to hit an opponent below the level of their belt.

He made a joke about her divorce which I thought was a bit below the belt.

by fair means or foul

If someone tries to achieve something by fair means or foul, they use any possible method to achieve it, not caring if their behaviour is dishonest or unfair.

They will do everything they can to win, by fair means or foul.

call a spade a spade

If you call a spade a spade, you speak honestly and directly about a subject even if it offends people.

NOTE   In a play by the Ancient Greek dramatist Menander, one of the characters says 'I call a fig a fig, and a spade a spade'.

In the meantime, Whyte is an outspoken voice who is willing to call a spade a spade.

come clean

If you come clean about something, you tell the truth about it.

I had expected her to come clean and confess that she only wrote these books for the money.

fair and square

If someone wins a competition or does something fair and square, they do it without cheating or lying.

My father bought them fair and square fifty years ago. We've still got the receipts.

keep your nose clean

If you keep your nose clean, you behave well and avoid trouble. [INFORMAL]

He'd worked hard and kept his nose clean for all those years.

lay your cards on the table or put your cards on the table

If you lay your cards on the table or put your cards on the table, you tell someone the truth about your feelings, opinions, or plans.

NOTE   Referring to when players in a card game lay their cards face up for the other players to see.

I'll lay my cards on the table: I think the new design is terrible.

I'm going to put my cards on the table and make you an offer.

a level playing field

A level playing field is a situation that is fair and where no one has an advantage over other people.

Trade with these nations must be conducted on a level playing field.

NOTE   You can also use even or uneven instead of level.

Given an even playing field, girls tend to do better at school than boys.

move the goalposts

If someone moves the goalposts, they change the rules or aims in a situation or activity, in order to gain an advantage and to make things more difficult for the other people involved.

They seem to move the goalposts every time I meet the required conditions.

NOTE   You can also say that someone shifts the goalposts.

The administration is shifting the goalposts and changing its demands.

on the level

Someone or something that is on the level is honest or true.

Wait a minute, something's odd here – is this guy on the level? Can we trust him?

stab someone in the back

If someone that you trust stabs you in the back, they secretly do something which hurts and betrays you.

She was incredibly disloyal. She would be your friend to your face, and then stab you in the back.

to someone's face

If you say something, especially something critical or unpleasant, to someone's face, you say it directly to them.

He was too old and he had to step aside. But who was going to say so to his face?

Exercise 1

Complete the sentences with the words in the box.

clean | board | level | belt | bush | table | means | nose

1 He's a good man who works hard and keeps his _____ clean.
2 I've decided I'm going to get that contract by fair _____ or foul.
3 I can offer you something better than that, and all on the _____.
4 I'll lay my cards on the _____: we've run out of money.
5 We suspect their deal was not entirely above _____.
6 She decided to come _____ and tell them exactly what had happened.
7 We feel these financial cuts are below the _____.
8 He's always very direct and never beats about the _____.

Exercise 2

Decide if the following sentences are true (*T*) or false (*F*).

1 If you lay your cards on the table, you are telling the truth. ☐
2 If something is above board, it's dishonest. ☐
3 If someone is on the level, you can't trust that person. ☐
4 If you move the goalposts, you make things easier for people. ☐
5 If you call a spade a spade, you are being direct. ☐
6 If you beat around the bush, you tell the truth immediately. ☐
7 If someone wins by fair means or foul, they are careful not to cheat. ☐
8 If a remark is below the belt, it is possibly true, but nevertheless painful. ☐

Exercise 3

Match sentence halves 1–8 with A–H to make complete sentences.

1 I'll lay my cards on the table
2 I can never please my manager –
3 The other candidates have more money than me
4 He won't say it to my face
5 It was horribly disappointing
6 If you keep your nose clean
7 He felt betrayed,
8 We should be honest

A because he's scared of me.
B and call a spade a spade.
C he always seems to be shifting the goalposts.
D and tell them that I've done all I can do.
E but we were beaten fair and square.
F as though his son had stabbed him in the back.
G you'll progress quickly in this company.
H so it's not a level playing field.

Exercise 4

Correct the idioms in these sentences.

1 I can guarantee that these are genuine. I bought them square and square from an antique dealer.
2 Stop beating around the field and tell the truth.
3 I think that comment about her personal life was below the bush. You should apologise to her.
4 Everyone should start from the beginning. That way, we have a level playing card for everyone.
5 If you have something to say, just be honest and say it to my back.
6 When his boss gave him a bad reference after all his hard work, it was a real stab in the face.
7 The deal was all legal and above the table.
8 His ambition is to get the top job, by square means or foul.

Exercise 5

Complete the sentences with idioms from this unit, changing the verb forms if necessary.

1 In all industries you need _____ to compete fairly with your competitors.
2 The world will never believe that he won that election _____.
3 Let's _____, we have to tell them exactly how we see it.
4 He needed to know to the truth, so she was going to go to his office and tell him _____.
5 If you _____ and tell us the truth, then it'll be a lot easier for you.
6 As soon as we reach a target, the management _____ and comes up with new demands.
7 'You'll be okay if you shut up and _____' he said.
8 She's determined to catch that criminal _____.

Exercise 6

Complete the table with idioms from this unit.

being direct	1 _____
	2 _____
	3 _____
	4 _____
being fair and honest	1 _____
	2 _____
	3 _____
	4 _____
	5 _____
	6 _____
not being fair or honest	1 _____
	2 _____
	3 _____

Your turn!

Think about your life recently. Use the idioms in this unit to describe your experiences with other people – when someone has or hasn't been very honest or fair, or when you have or haven't been very direct. For example:

When Carlo told me our class was cancelled, I wasn't sure he was on the level.

I had to come clean *and tell my boss that I was going to miss the deadline.*

Jim didn't like the way the man was talking to him but decided not to say anything **to his face.**

Deception

blow the whistle on someone/something

If you blow the whistle on something dishonest or illegal, or on someone who is doing something dishonest or illegal, you tell the authorities about them because you feel strongly that what they are doing is wrong.

NOTE   In games such as football, the referee blows a whistle to stop play when a player has committed a foul (=an act that is not allowed).

Members of coastal communities are being asked to blow the whistle on activities that damage the marine environment.

cover your tracks

If someone covers their tracks, they hide or destroy evidence of what they have done or where they have been.

NOTE   Tracks here mean footprints.

He was a very clever man who never took a chance, a man who always covered his tracks.

be economical with the truth

If someone is economical with the truth, they deceive people by not telling them the whole truth about something.

When they insisted that no changes had been made to the original plan, his team was being economical with the truth.

give the game away

If someone or something gives the game away, they reveal something which someone had been trying to keep secret.

Eric had intended to make his announcement in an article in The Times but the paper gave the game away by advertising the article a week before publishing.

go behind someone's back

If someone goes behind your back, they do something secretly or without your permission.

Do you think I wouldn't know if you went behind my back?

go through the motions

If you go through the motions, you do something that you have to do or are expected to do, but without any real effort or enthusiasm.

Alex didn't really care about his job anymore, he was just going through the motions.

a hidden agenda

If someone has a hidden agenda, they are secretly trying to achieve something while they appear to be doing something else.

NOTE   An agenda is a list of things that need to be dealt with, for example at a meeting.

The unions fear these tactics are part of a hidden agenda to reduce pay and conditions throughout the company.

keep something under your hat

If you keep something under your hat, you do not tell anyone else about it. [INFORMAL]

NOTE   This was a slogan used to promote security in Britain during the Second World War.

Very few people know, so keep it under your hat.

lead someone up the garden path

If someone leads you up the garden path, they deceive you by making you believe something which is not true.

He led me up the garden path. He said their relationship was over but now I know that it wasn't.

lie through your teeth

If someone lies through their teeth, they tell obvious lies and do not seem to be embarrassed about this.

We ought to be angry that public officials lie through their teeth.

on the fiddle

If someone is on the fiddle, they are getting money dishonestly, for example by cheating with the accounts at work. [BRITISH]

A postman earning only £136 a week drove around in a Porsche for six months before his bosses realized he was on the fiddle.

pull someone's leg

If you pull someone's leg, you tease them about something, for example by telling them something which is not true.

NOTE   There are two possible explanations for this expression, although there is no proof for either. One suggestion is that in the past, when someone was being hanged, their friends or family sometimes pulled their legs hard so that they died more quickly and suffered less. Alternatively, the expression may refer to thieves tripping people up before they robbed them.

Tracey hasn't really got a new job in New York. She was just pulling your leg.

sweep something under the carpet

If you sweep a problem under the carpet, you try to hide it and forget about it. [BRITISH]

People often hope that if they sweep something under the carpet the problem will go away, but that is not the case.

NOTE   You can also use verbs such as brush and push instead of sweep.

The problem has been brushed under the carpet for decades.

a white lie

If you tell a white lie, you say something which is untrue, often in order to protect someone or to avoid upsetting someone.

I said she looked nice, thinking it kinder to tell a white lie.

Exercise 1

Complete the sentences. Choose the best answers.

1 I never know if he's serious or if he's pulling my _____.

   a leg   b teeth   c hat

2 It's obvious that she's lying through her _____.

   a hat   b teeth   c back

3 This information is too important, you can't sweep it under the _____.

   a tracks   b carpet   c back

4 Please keep this story under your _____.

   a leg   b carpet   c hat

5 They made careful plans and carefully covered their _____.

   a tracks   b back   c carpet

6 I was surprised to find he'd gone behind my _____.

   a hat   b back   c leg

Exercise 2

Match idioms 1–6 with situations A–F.

1 She wasn't enjoying herself so she said she was too tired to stay.

2 He hated parties but he went anyway.

3 We found out after she left that she'd been taking money from the till.

4 The company offered him a 'free' holiday weekend and then tried to sell him the apartment.

5 We knew she was guilty when she started to cry.

6 They stole some cash and she told the manager.

A She was on the fiddle.

B She gave the game away.

C She blew the whistle on them.

D He went through the motions.

E She told a white lie.

F They had a hidden agenda.

Exercise 3

Match sentence halves 1–6 with A–F to make complete sentences.

1 When you mentioned seeing her at the surprise party

2 I'm not really enthusiastic about the trip –

3 They thought they'd get away with it but someone

4 He never seems to get caught for his dishonesty – he's

5 I can see they're not telling the truth – they're

6 When they mentioned a pay rise they were

A good at covering his tracks.

B you really gave the game away!

C leading me up the garden path.

D lying through their teeth.

E blew the whistle on them.

F I'm just going through the motions.

Exercise 4

Correct the idioms in these sentences.

1 Many of the politicians were found to be pulling the fiddle.

2 She looks twenty years younger than she really is. Only the skin on her hands blows the game away.

3 Look, if I tell you something will you promise to cover it under your hat?

4 The week he died, the Foreign Minister was planning to blow the fiddle on corrupt top-level officials.

5 The killer may return to the scene of the crime to brush away his tracks.

6 Ministers and heads of industry are going under the motions of negotiating with the unions.

Exercise 5

Complete the sentences with the words in the box.

> keep it under your hat | pulling your leg | economical with the truth | on the fiddle | a white lie
> led us up the garden path | a hidden agenda | go behind my back

1 His business was closed down after it was discovered that he hadn't been declaring all his earnings – he'd been _____.
2 I wonder what the real purpose of this meeting is? I suspect there's _____.
3 When she asked me what I thought of her new hairstyle, I decided not to hurt her feelings and told _____.
4 Don't take him seriously – he's only _____.
5 It was very dishonest of you to _____ and gossip about me to others.
6 Please don't tell anyone about my new job just yet – _____.
7 The newspapers have _____ on this matter.
8 He said there was no point being honest when you could make so much more money being _____.

Exercise 6

Complete the table. Put the idioms in the correct groups.

> blow the whistle on someone | a white lie | a hidden agenda | give the game away
> pull someone's leg | go through the motions | be economical with the truth
> sweep something under the carpet

lying	1 _____
	2 _____
pretending	1 _____
	2 _____
hiding the truth	1 _____
	2 _____
telling the truth	1 _____
	2 _____

Your turn!

Have you heard, seen, or been involved in any kind of deception recently? Use the idioms in this unit to describe your experience. For example:

I told a white lie when I said I didn't mind that my friend forgot my birthday.

It was clear that Pablo was lying through his teeth when he said he'd left his homework on the kitchen table.

She was extremely bored, but decided to **go through the motions.**

12

Anger and irritation

bite someone's head off or snap someone's head off

If someone bites your head off or snaps your head off, they speak to you in an unpleasant, angry way, because they are annoyed about something. [INFORMAL]

Don't bite my head off just because you're fed up!

blow a fuse

If you blow a fuse, you suddenly lose your temper and cannot control your anger.

> NOTE A fuse is a safety device found in electrical equipment. If the equipment becomes too hot, the fuse blows, or burns. This breaks the electrical circuit, so that the equipment will stop working.

He's going to blow a fuse when he finds out about Miller.

a dirty look or a filthy look

If someone gives you a dirty look or a filthy look, they look at you in a way that shows that they are very angry about something.

Tony was being really annoying. Michael gave him a dirty look and walked out of the kitchen.

drive someone up the wall

If something or someone drives you up the wall, they annoy you very much. [INFORMAL]

He's so uncooperative he's beginning to drive me up the wall.

a face like thunder

If someone has a face like thunder, they look extremely angry. [BRITISH]

The kitchen had flooded and Mick was raging around the house with a face like thunder.

fly off the handle

If you fly off the handle, you suddenly become very angry. [INFORMAL]

> NOTE The reference here is to an axe head (=the metal cutting part) which has become loose, and so when someone swings the axe, the axe head flies off.

When I finally managed to speak to him, he flew off the handle and shouted down the phone.

give someone hell

1 If someone gives you hell, they make your life very unpleasant by behaving badly towards you.

Their younger son gives them hell.

2 If you say that someone gives you hell, they shout at you or speak to you angrily because you have done something wrong.

I got home three hours late and my mum gave me hell.

go through the roof or hit the roof

If someone goes through the roof or hits the roof, they suddenly become very angry, and usually show their anger by shouting at someone. [INFORMAL]

When I told my mother she went through the roof.

She took one look at my hair and hit the roof.

have a chip on your shoulder

If someone has a chip on their shoulder, they feel angry and resentful because they think that they have been treated unfairly, especially because of their background. [SPOKEN]

> NOTE   A 'chip' is a small piece that has been broken off something larger. There is a story that in America in the past, men sometimes balanced a small piece of wood on one shoulder in the hope that someone would knock it off and give them an excuse to start a fight.

She thinks he has a chip on his shoulder *because he didn't go to university.*

have a fit or throw a fit

If someone has a fit or throws a fit, they become very angry and upset.

Mum will have a fit *when she hears about this.*

She threw a fit *when she found me in the dressing room.*

lose it

If someone loses it, they become extremely angry or upset. [INFORMAL]

I completely lost it. *I was shouting and swearing.*

make your blood boil

If something makes your blood boil, it makes you very angry.

> NOTE   In medieval times, some people believed that certain emotions changed the temperature of the blood.

It makes my blood boil. *He doesn't like talking to the players but he wants his opinions known.*

a pain in the neck

If someone or something is a pain in the neck, they are very annoying. [INFORMAL]

He was a pain in the neck. *I was glad when he left my department.*

'Sorry,' he said. 'They've forgotten to insure the car. It's a pain in the neck, but what can I do?'

a sore point or a sore spot

You can say that a subject is a sore point with someone or a sore spot for them if it makes them feel angry, embarrassed, or upset.

The continuing presence of foreign troops remains a very sore point *with these students.*

Slow job growth is a sore spot *for the President.*

> NOTE   If you touch or hit someone's sore point or sore spot, you mention a subject which makes them feel angry, embarrassed, or upset.

The mention of Jim Kennerly had touched her sore spot.

It was clear by his expression that my question had hit a sore point.

Exercise 1

Find four idioms that have the same meaning.

1 Elisa's parents hit the roof when she crashed their car.
2 Our teacher was clearly getting angry, then suddenly she blew a fuse.
3 Everyone finds the new student a complete pain in the neck.
4 Kenji finally lost it when his laptop crashed again.
5 I don't want to tell you because I'm sure you'll throw a fit.
6 Don't mention English grades because Jonas has a chip on his shoulder after doing badly last year.

Exercise 2

Complete the sentences with the words in the box.

| up | on | in | off | through | off |

1 His stupid jokes drive me _____ the wall.
2 My sister will go _____ the roof when she finds out.
3 I was surprised when she bit my head _____.
4 Lourdes is always flying _____ the handle at her husband.
5 There's a boy in our class who's a real pain _____ the neck.
6 I think you've got a bit of a chip _____ your shoulder.

Exercise 3

Match sentence halves 1–8 with A–H to make complete sentences.

1 Majid gave me a filthy look

2 Driving lessons are Paula's sore spot because
3 Mum always has a fit when
4 My boss often snaps my head off when
5 My friends will give me hell if
6 It drives me up the wall
7 She had a face like thunder,
8 Dora makes my blood boil,

A to hear Viktor talking about all his successful business deals.
B we're understaffed and I'm late for work.
C the way she never thanks me for my help.
D so I asked her what was wrong.
E she's failed her test four times.
F I keep them waiting yet again.
G we don't clean the kitchen properly.
H to shut me up.

Exercise 4

Re-order the phrases to make sentences. Add punctuation where necessary.

1 a dirty look for / his brother / Dmitri gave / laughing
2 with Cynthia / is a sore point / Virginia's engagement
3 gave us hell / what we'd done / the headmaster / when he found out
4 if you promise / I'll only tell you / not to blow a fuse
5 borrow her bike again / fly off the handle / if you ask to / Clara is likely to
6 when / he hit the roof / the mess / Dad discovered
7 the knowledge that / of this crime / he is guilty / makes my blood boil
8 marching out of the room / I saw / with a face like thunder / Mr Clarke come

Exercise 5

Match words 1–6 with phrases A–F to make idioms from this unit.

1 blow
2 bite
3 drive
4 fly
5 make
6 have

A your blood boil
B off the handle
C a fuse
D someone up the wall
E a chip on your shoulder
F someone's head off

Work on your Idioms Anger and irritation

Exercise 6

Correct the idioms in these sentences.

1 It makes my head boil just to think about the way he spoke to me.
2 When I arrived he was sitting in the chair with a look like thunder.
3 I asked him how he was, and he just bit my neck off!
4 She looked really upset when I said that. I must have hit a sore shoulder.
5 He's got a fiery temper. He flies off the fuse for the smallest reason.
6 I can't stand it when he does that. It drives me up the roof!
7 That boy is really irritating. He's a pain in the head.
8 When I mentioned the incident, he gave me such a filthy chip.

Exercise 7

Choose the most appropriate thing A–H to say in each situation 1–8.

1 Someone is really annoying you.
2 You think someone has a deep resentment about a family member.
3 You find a particular task really tiresome and annoying.
4 You are talking about a teenager you know who really makes his mother's life difficult.
5 Someone has looked at you in a way to suggest they are angry with you.
6 You realize you have reacted strongly to someone because they've mentioned something you feel quite emotional about.
7 A teacher is looking angrily at the students in his classroom.
8 Your friend tells you to shut up when you enter the room and say hello.

A It's a pain in the neck.
B You're driving me up the wall.
C Why did you give me a dirty look?
D There's no need to snap my head off.
E He has a face like thunder.
F I think you've got a chip on your shoulder.
G I'm sorry. It's just that you hit a sore spot when you said that.
H He gives his mother hell.

Your turn!

Have you been angry or irritated recently? Use the idioms in this unit to describe your experience.
For example:

I think my boss is a pain in the neck.

I lost it when Zul dropped my mobile phone.

Unfortunately, he hadn't noticed the **filthy looks** he was getting.

Fear and frustration

at the end of your tether

If you are at the end of your tether, you are very upset because you are no longer able to deal with a difficult situation.

> NOTE   A tether is a rope or chain which is used to tie an animal to a post or fence.

I had tried every solution I could think of. I was at the end of my tether.

a bundle of nerves

If you say that someone is a bundle of nerves, you mean that they are extremely nervous.

> NOTE   A bundle is a number of things that are tied or wrapped together.

Elaine admitted she was a bundle of nerves when she had to sing in front of the queen.

butterflies in your stomach

If you have butterflies in your stomach, you feel very nervous about something that you have to do.

Now I've qualified as a competitor, I'm starting to feel the butterflies in my stomach already.

> NOTE   Butterflies is also used in many other structures and expressions with a similar meaning.

If a jockey says he doesn't get butterflies down at the start, he's telling lies.

frighten the life out of someone or scare the life out of someone

If someone or something frightens the life out of you or scares the life out of you, they frighten you very much. [INFORMAL]

It used to frighten the life out of me when they tried to jump on the moving train.

Further tests revealed that I needed major heart surgery. It scared the life out of me.

get cold feet or have cold feet

If you get cold feet or have cold feet about something you have planned to do, you become nervous about it and are not sure that you want to do it.

Leaving Ireland wasn't easy and I had cold feet about it a couple of times.

not get a word in edgeways

If you cannot get a word in edgeways in a conversation, you find it difficult to say anything because someone else is talking so much. [BRITISH]

For heaven's sake, Sue, will you let me get a word in edgeways!

give someone the creeps

If someone or something gives you the creeps, they make you feel nervous or frightened. [INFORMAL]

That statue in my parents' hallway always gave me the creeps.

jump out of your skin or nearly jump out of your skin

If you jump out of your skin or nearly jump out of your skin, you are suddenly very surprised or shocked by something.

The first time I heard shots I jumped out of my skin but now I hardly notice them.

I was concentrating so hard I nearly jumped out of my skin when there was a sudden knock on the door.

the last straw or the final straw

If you say that something is the last straw or the final straw, you mean it is the latest in a series of bad events and it makes you unable to deal with a situation any longer.

NOTE   The reference here is to an animal which is already carrying a great deal on its back and which collapses when one more thing is added.

The relationship had been in trouble for a while and Jack's behaviour that night was just the final straw.

on edge

If someone is on edge, they are anxious and unable to relax.

She seemed a bit on edge the whole evening, which I decided was due to work stress.

red tape

Red tape is official rules and documents that seem unnecessary and cause delay.

NOTE   Lawyers and government officials used to tie documents together with red or pink tape.

After dealing with all the red tape and finally getting approval for the building, our funding has been cut.

scare someone out of their wits

If something or someone scares you out of your wits, they make you very frightened or worried.

Oh, I'm so glad you're all right! You scared us out of our wits. We heard you had an accident.

NOTE   The verb frighten is sometimes used instead of scare.

The tree crashed through the conservatory, frightening me out of my wits.

be shaking like a leaf

If someone is shaking like a leaf, their body is shaking a lot, usually because they are very frightened.

I didn't think about the danger at the time. Afterwards I was shaking like a leaf.

until you are blue in the face

If you say that someone can say or do something until they are blue in the face, you mean that however many times they say or do it, it will have no effect. [INFORMAL]

The president can issue orders until he is blue in the face, but no one will take any notice.

Exercise 1

Choose the best answer to complete the sentences.

1 I had _____ in my stomach before I walked out onto the stage.

   a creeps   b butterflies   c nerves

2 I've written to the newspapers until I'm blue in the _____ but they do nothing.

   a face   b skin   c feet

3 The door suddenly banged and frightened the _____ out of me.

   a life   b leaf   c wits

4 After the car alarm went off, getting the key stuck in the lock was the last _____.

   a edge   b straw   c word

5 I'm at the end of my _____ – I can't find my credit card anywhere.

   a tether   b mind   c nerves

6 Could you please stop for a moment and let me get a _____ in edgeways?

   a straw   b foot   c word

Exercise 2

Choose the correct explanation for each sentence.

1 There was so much red tape involved in getting a visa.

   a It was expensive.   b There were a lot of official documents to complete.

2 I'm at the end of my tether.

   a I've really had enough of this situation.   b I'm finished my task.

3 I nearly jumped out of my skin!

   a Something made me laugh.   b I was frightened.

4 I've got butterflies in my stomach.

   a I feel ill.   b I am nervous.

5 Just before the parachute jump, I got cold feet.

   a I was too scared to do it.   b I couldn't wait to do it.

6 What's wrong? You're shaking like a leaf.

   a I think you've got some exciting news to tell me.   b I think you've had some shocking news.

Exercise 3

Match sentence halves 1–6 with A–F to make complete sentences.

1 She's afraid of flying. Before the plane takes off	A He just gives me the creeps, for some reason.
2 Please take off that horrible mask.	B I´ve been on edge about work – things are very stressful at the moment.
3 I don't know why I feel uneasy about that man.	C it was the last straw!
4 You've had a nasty shock. Sit down –	D she's a bundle of nerves.
5 I'm sorry I've been in such a bad mood recently.	E You scared me out of my wits!
6 I was late for work – and then when I tripped on the way to the bus stop	F you're shaking like a leaf.

Exercise 4

Correct the idioms in these sentences.

1 He was on the edge, continually glancing behind him, thinking he was being followed.

2 When his phone rang, he almost jumped out of his stomach.

3 The house was silent and still and gave me the cold creeps.

4 She was frightened out of her tether, but somehow managed to swim back to shore and crawl out of the water.

5 On the morning of the match I was a bunch of nerves.

6 Poor Charles was totally exhausted and just about at the end of his wits.

Exercise 5

Complete the sentences with idioms from this unit, changing the pronouns and verb forms if necessary. Some sentences can take more than one idiom.

1   I nearly _____ when the plate crashed to the floor.
2   Ingrid felt _____, wondering what he would think of her family and her house.
3   I argued _____ that the project was worth the money, but no one would listen.
4   Immediately after the accident, as I realised I was still alive, I noticed that I _____.
5   When they told me I'd got the part, I suddenly _____ and nearly changed my mind.
6   We are spending more and more time dealing with _____ and filling in forms.
7   It was _____: he snatched his coat and marched out of the office.
8   The way she carefully studied me and took my personal details _____.

Exercise 6

Complete the table. Put the idioms in the correct groups.

a bundle of nerves | not get a word in edgeways | jump out of your skin | butterflies in your stomach
frighten the life out of someone | at the end of your tether | scare someone out of their wits
get/have cold feet

sudden fright	1	_____
	2	_____
	3	_____
feeling nervous	1	_____
	2	_____
	3	_____
frustration	1	_____
	2	_____

Your turn!

Have you felt fear, nervousness, or frustration recently? Use the idioms in this unit to describe your experience. For example:

The fire alarm went off during class and scared the life out of us.

I was a bundle of nerves before my oral exam.

The bird was **the last straw.**

Disagreement

agree to differ or agree to disagree

If two people who are arguing about something agree to differ or agree to disagree, they decide to stop arguing because neither of them is going to change their opinion.

I find some of his views very odd and we've agreed to differ on some things.

You and I are going to have to agree to disagree on this issue.

at each other's throats or at one another's throats

If two people or groups are at each other's throats or at one another's throats, they are arguing in a very angry way.

The politicians are at one another's throats all the time, and are not functioning as a very effective government.

a battle of wills

If an argument or conflict is a battle of wills, the person with the strongest beliefs or personality will win.

NOTE   Someone's will is their determination to do something.

It was a battle of wills, and Grace's was the stronger.

a bone of contention

A bone of contention is an issue that people are arguing about.

NOTE   The image here is of two dogs fighting over a bone.

Pay, of course, is not the only bone of contention.

clear the air

If something such as an argument or a discussion clears the air, it makes bad feelings between people go away.

I get angry with Hannah, but I'm a great believer in expressing my feelings to clear the air.

cross swords

If you cross swords with someone, you disagree and argue with them or oppose them.

He repeatedly crossed swords with the Prime Minister in the early 1970s.

fight like cat and dog

If two people fight like cat and dog, they frequently have violent arguments or fights with each other.

My brother and I are very close in age and we used to fight like cat and dog.

give someone a piece of your mind

If you give someone a piece of your mind, you speak angrily to them because they have done something to annoy you. [INFORMAL]

You can't let people get away with behaviour like that. You should have given her a piece of your mind*!*

have a bone to pick with someone

If you say that you have a bone to pick with someone, you mean that you are annoyed with them about something, and you want to talk to them about it. [INFORMAL]

NOTE   This expression may refer to the fact that dogs often fight over bones.

'I have a bone to pick with you'. She wanted to bring up a matter that she had been afraid to discuss before.

have a go at someone

If you have a go at someone, you criticize them strongly, often without good reason. [mainly BRITISH, INFORMAL]

I was angry because I figured she was just having a go at me *for the sake of it.*

in someone's bad books

If you are in someone's bad books, you have done something that has annoyed them. [BRITISH, INFORMAL]

Thomas knew that having burnt the cakes, he would be in Mrs Simpson's bad books*.*

jump down someone's throat

If someone jumps down your throat, they react in a very angry way to something you have said or done. [INFORMAL]

If I even asked her about her day, she'd jump down my throat*, as if I were interrogating her.*

kiss and make up

If two people or groups kiss and make up, they become friends again after an argument or fight.

I sent her a big bottle of champagne with a note saying, 'Sorry, hope we can kiss and make up*'.*

not see eye to eye

If you do not see eye to eye with someone, you do not agree with them about something.

The Prime Minister didn't see eye to eye *with him on this issue.*

NOTE   You can also say that you see eye to eye with someone, meaning that you agree with them about something.

Yes, we argue about stuff but see eye to eye on the important issues.

a shouting match

A shouting match is an angry and uncontrolled argument or discussion about something, usually involving shouting.

For a moment I thought the meeting was going to become a shouting match*.*

Exercise 1

Complete the sentences with the words in the box.

bone | shouting | throats | differ | pick | fight | air | kiss

1 The argument began to develop into a noisy _____ match.
2 The date of the wedding became a _____ of contention between the two families.
3 They each felt strongly about the issue and finally agreed to _____.
4 It's common for brothers and sisters to _____ like cat and dog in their teens.
5 They argue constantly but always manage to _____ and make up.
6 I've got a bone to _____ with you! Why have you been avoiding me?
7 The children were constantly at each other's _____ during the school holidays.
8 I finally managed to explain what really happened and that cleared the _____.

Exercise 2

Match sentence halves 1–8 with A–H to make complete sentences.

1 If I'd been the parent,
2 I've had a long day, I'm exhausted and fed up
3 She liked him a lot but
4 There's no need to jump down my throat

5 I have crossed swords a number of times
6 The battle of wills may go on for some time
7 A major bone of contention between them
8 Let's just stop arguing about it

A they rarely saw eye to eye on things.
B with my boss.
C and agree to differ, shall we?
D and you have a go at me as soon as I walk in the door.
E I'd have given the teacher a piece of my mind.
F was whether they should buy a car.
G as neither child wants to lose the argument.
H when I try to make a helpful suggestion.

Exercise 3

Match situations 1–6 with explanations A–F.

1 They see eye to eye on most matters.
2 They went to a dinner party that turned into a shouting match.
3 They usually end up agreeing to disagree.
4 They take every opportunity to have a go at each other.
5 They fight like cat and dog when they are alone.
6 They avoid crossing swords if possible.

A They frequently criticize one another.
B They try not to argue with one another.
C They generally agree about things.
D They finish their arguments in a friendly way.
E They have violent arguments at home.
F They were among guests who argued.

Exercise 4

Complete the sentences. Choose the best answers.

1 We've discussed the issue but still have different views. We'll have to *kiss and make up / agree to differ / cross swords*.
2 When we were younger, my sister and I used to *fight like cat and dog / have a bone of contention / have a bone to pick*.
3 I only asked you how your test was! There was no need for you to *have a battle of wills / jump down my throat / have a shouting match*!
4 I was really annoyed, so when I phoned customer services I *had a bone of contention with them / saw eye to eye with them / gave them a piece of my mind*.
5 He has a very bad temper. I wouldn't like to *cross swords / fight like cat and dog / kiss and make up* with him.
6 I've got *a bone of contention / bone to pick with you / battle of wills with you* – why did you borrow my phone without asking me?
7 I decided to have a long calm talk with her to *have a go at her / cross swords with her / clear the air*.
8 The moment I saw him I knew I was *in his bad books / seeing eye to eye with him / a bone of contention*.

Work on your Idioms Disagreement

Exercise 5

Re-order the phrases to make sentences. Add punctuation where necessary.

1 about / my work / had a go at me / my boss
2 don't / about politics / we / see eye to eye
3 many families / often / a bone of contention in / housework is
4 can be / getting children / their homework / a battle of wills / to do
5 kiss and make up / argue a lot / they / but always
6 to turn into / don't want / I / a shouting match / this discussion
7 the right moment / until she found / to clear the air / she waited
8 in my teacher's bad books / I was / doing my homework / for not

Exercise 6

Correct the idioms in these sentences.

1 She and the Director General could hear eye to eye on this matter.
2 How can we discuss this properly when you are always at one another's eyes?
3 You could at least listen before you shout down my throat.
4 The score was five all and the football match became a battle of bones.
5 She felt that she wanted to give those decision makers a go at her mind.
6 It's important for the economy that the two leaders should give and make up.
7 I guess almost everyone has a match to pick with the government.
8 The young man's ambition to become an actor was a battle of contention between him and his father.

Your turn!

Use the idioms in this unit to describe any disagreements you have had with your friends, your classmates, colleagues, or family. For example:

I don't like crossing swords with anyone if I can avoid it.

I don't see eye to eye with my parents about my future.

They agreed on most things, but on their taste in fashion, they had to **agree to differ**.

Success and failure

back to the drawing board

If you have to go back to the drawing board, something you have done has not been successful and you have to try another idea.

> NOTE   Drawing boards are large flat boards, on which designers or architects place their paper when drawing plans.

His government should go back to the drawing board *to rethink their programme.*

bring the house down

If a person or their performance brings the house down, the audience claps and cheers loudly for a long time because they liked the performance so much.

> NOTE   In this expression, the 'house' means a theatre.

We had just one rehearsal and I was very nervous but the show brought the house down.

come up in the world

If someone has come up in the world, they are richer or more powerful than they used to be and have a higher social status.

A polite and pleasant young man, he was an ordinary worker who had come up in the world.

> NOTE   You can also say that someone has gone up in the world or moved up in the world.

fall flat on your face

If someone falls flat on their face when they try to do something, they fail or make an embarrassing mistake.

He was trying to introduce changes in the prison system but he fell flat on his face.

be fighting a losing battle

If you are fighting a losing battle, you are trying to achieve something, but you are very unlikely to succeed.

The theatre has to compete with the movies and DVDs and it's fighting a losing battle.

go belly-up

If a company goes belly-up, it fails and does not have enough money to pay its debts. [INFORMAL]

> NOTE   This expression may refer to dead fish floating upside down near the surface of the water.

Factories and farms went belly-up *because of the debt crisis.*

go pear-shaped

If a situation or activity goes pear-shaped, it starts to fail or have problems. [BRITISH, INFORMAL]

He is always asked to comment when the global economy goes pear-shaped.

hit the nail on the head

If you hit the nail on the head, you describe a situation or problem very precisely.

Smith hit the nail on the head when he said that the Prime Minister promised so much and yet changed so little.

plain sailing

If an activity or task is plain sailing, it is easy to do or achieve. [BRITISH]

NOTE   'Plain sailing' is sailing in good conditions, without any difficulties. However, the expression may have come from 'plane sailing', a method of working out the position of a ship and planning its route using calculations based on the earth being flat rather than round. This is a simple and easy method which is fairly accurate over short distances, especially near the equator.

Once I got used to the diet it was plain sailing and I lost six kilos over a four-month period.

save the day

If someone or something saves the day in a situation which seems likely to fail, they manage to make it successful.

After a disastrous first night for the show, it was Biggs who stepped in to save the day.

touch and go

If it is touch and go whether something will happen, you cannot be certain whether it will happen or not.

I thought I was going to win the race, but it was still touch and go.

win hands down

If you win a contest hands down, you win it easily.

NOTE   This expression was originally used in horse racing to describe jockeys who won their races very easily and could cross the winning line with their hands lowered and the reins (=thin leather straps attached around a horse's neck) loose.

We have been beaten in some games which we should have won hands down.

NOTE   You can also say that you beat someone else hands down.

When he said he would beat me hands down, I didn't know he could run that fast!

with flying colours

If you achieve something, such as passing an examination, with flying colours, you achieve it easily and are very successful.

NOTE   The image here is of a ship that has won a battle, sailing back into port with its colours (=a military flag) flying.

She passed the entrance exam with flying colours.

work like a charm

If something works like a charm, it is very successful or effective.

Our little arrangement worked like a charm.

Exercise 1

Choose the best answer to complete the sentences.

1 I'm sure you'll pass your final exam with flying _____.

   a flags   **b** colours   **c** sails

2 She guessed – and hit the _____ on the head first time.

   a nail   **b** board   **c** hammer

3 It seemed like a good idea but I fell _____ on my face.

   a down   **b** belly-up   **c** flat

4 I'm trying to learn Japanese but I think I'm fighting a losing _____.

   a fight   **b** battle   **c** face

5 That nail varnish remover you gave me worked like a _____.

   a charm   **b** pear   **c** trick

6 We've done the hard work – it'll be _____ sailing from now on.

   a plain   **b** flying   **c** flat

7 The plan went _____-shaped almost from the very start.

   a belly   **b** face   **c** pear

8 All my work over the last year has just gone _____!

   a belly-up   **b** down   **c** flat

Exercise 2

Decide if the sentences are true (*T*) or false (*F*).

1 If a performance brings the house down, it is a complete failure. ☐
2 If someone saves the day, they make it a success. ☐
3 If something goes belly-up, it fails. ☐
4 If something goes pear-shaped, it goes according to plan. ☐
5 If you have to go back to the drawing board, you have to start again. ☐
6 If something works like a charm, it doesn't have the desired results. ☐
7 If you hit the nail on the head, you are wrong about something. ☐
8 If something is touch and go, the outcome is certain. ☐

Exercise 3

Re-order the phrases to make sentences. Add punctuation where necessary.

1 will win the final / we're hoping / hands down / that our team
2 to go belly-up / the exporters / it looks like / are likely
3 for the launch of / all our arrangements / the new products / have gone pear-shaped
4 move up in the world / can expect to / a keen young politician / who knows the right people
5 be prepared to go / we have to / to fix these serious problems / back to the drawing board
6 would be / it was touch and go / finished in time / whether my manuscript

Exercise 4

Correct the idioms in these sentences.

1 Our presentation started off well, but then it all went flat-shaped at the end.
2 That's it! You've really hit the head on the nail.
3 Being a student is not all plain playing – there's a lot of hard work to do.
4 He's really come up in the face since his humble beginnings.
5 Our team was far better than the competition and we won hands up.
6 It was start and go as to whether he would survive the accident – but he's made a full recovery.

Exercise 5

Complete the sentences with idioms from this unit, changing the verb forms if necessary.

1 Once I've done the research, writing the report will be _____.
2 I agree with you entirely. I think you've _____.
3 We started well, but it all _____ and we lost five matches in a row.
4 The medicine _____ and my life has greatly improved.
5 I told myself I was going to try even harder and I would not _____ again.
6 The newspapers _____ to maintain their sales figures.
7 Mr Cheng's secretary finally found the missing documents and _____.
8 The audience loved her dancing and her performance _____.

Exercise 6

Complete the table with idioms from this unit.

success	1 _____
	2 _____
	3 _____
	4 _____
	5 _____
	6 _____
	7 _____
	8 _____
failure	1 _____
	2 _____
	3 _____
	4 _____
	5 _____
neither success nor failure	1 _____

Your turn!

Use the idioms in this unit to describe any experiences of success or failure that you've had recently. For example:

I didn't exactly pass my exam with flying colours *but I did okay.*

My flatmate beat me hands down *at tennis yesterday.*

The sailor felt he was making progress, but really was just **fighting a losing battle**.

Progress

be barking up the wrong tree

If someone is barking up the wrong tree, they are following the wrong course of action because their beliefs about something are not correct.

> NOTE   This expression comes from raccoon (=a small long-tailed animal in North and Central America) hunting, which takes place at night. Dogs that are trained to show where raccoons are by barking sometimes indicate the wrong tree.

Scientists in Switzerland realized that most other researchers had been barking up the wrong tree.

be flogging a dead horse

If someone is flogging a dead horse, they are wasting their time trying to achieve something that cannot be done. [BRITISH]

After all our hard work, we don't seem to be making any progress. It feels like we're flogging a dead horse – it's all very discouraging.

gain ground

If something or someone gains ground, they make progress and become more important or more powerful.

His ideas on nutrition have been gaining ground in recent years.

> NOTE   The opposite of gain ground is lose ground.

get to grips with something or come to grips with something

If you get to grips with or come to grips with a problem or task, you start to deal with it effectively, usually by making an effort to understand it.

The present government has completely failed to get to grips with our economic problems.

I must come to grips with this new system.

get your act together

If you get your act together, you organize yourself effectively so that you can deal successfully with things. [INFORMAL]

We're going to be 22 points behind by Monday and we've got to get our act together.

go around in circles or go round in circles

If someone goes around in circles or goes round in circles, they achieve little because they repeatedly deal with the same point or problem.

This was one of those debates which simply went round in circles.

My mind was going around in circles, worrying, but I knew that no news was good news.

in the doldrums

If a person, organization, economy, etc. is in the doldrums, they are not successful and are not making any progress.

NOTE This expression relates to the Doldrums, which is an area of sea near the equator where there is often little or no wind. This meant that sailing ships could be stuck there for long periods.

The restaurant business, like many other businesses, is in the doldrums.

in the pipeline

If something is in the pipeline, it is being planned or developed.

NOTE A pipeline is a large pipe that carries oil or gas over a long distance, often underground.

Another development in the pipeline is closed-circuit TV cameras in most stores.

light at the end of the tunnel

If there is light at the end of the tunnel, there is hope that a difficult situation might be coming to an end.

After a very difficult time we are seeing light at the end of the tunnel.

make headway

If you make headway, you make progress with something that you are trying to achieve.

A spokesman said the two sides have made headway on some issues.

on a roll

If you are on a roll, you are making great progress and having a lot of success.

NOTE This expression probably comes from surfing.

I'd done my first deal and I was on a roll, I couldn't see anything going wrong.

NOTE You can say that someone gets on a roll.

Once you get on a roll you feel as though you're unbeatable.

on the right track

If someone or something is on the right track, they are acting or developing in a way that is likely to be successful.

We are finding that guests for lunch and dinner are returning in increasing numbers – a sure sign that we are on the right track.

NOTE The opposite of on the right track is on the wrong track.

put something on hold

If you put something on hold, you decide not to do it or deal with it until a later time.

NOTE This expression is probably from the term used in the past when someone making a telephone call waited for the operator to connect them.

We'll have to put the project on hold until we get some more money.

NOTE You can also just say that something is on hold.

A few months later it was announced that the deal was on hold, perhaps permanently.

Exercise 1

Complete the sentences with the words in the box.

| doldrums | hold | horse | track | ground | act |

1 I was bored and my career was in the _____.
2 Yoga for children is something that seems to be gaining _____.
3 He has had no success with this idea. I think he's flogging a dead _____.
4 At least this result tells us that we're on the right _____.
5 If we want this plan to succeed we must get our _____ together right now.
6 The building development has been put on _____ because of financial problems.

Exercise 2

Choose the best definition for each sentence.

1 He's on a roll.

   a making progress and having success   b getting confused

2 Video conferencing is gaining ground in the workplace.

   a becoming less popular   b becoming more popular

3 Could you read my draft essay and tell me if I'm on the right track?

   a developing it in the right way   b got everything right first time

4 We're going round in circles on this issue.

   a coming to a conclusion   b not making any progress

5 I'm struggling to get to grips with this equipment.

   a can't hold it correctly   b don't understand it properly

6 After a lot of research we came to the conclusion that we'd been barking up the wrong tree.

   a misunderstanding the situation   b doing too much work

Exercise 3

Match sentence halves 1–6 with A–F to make complete sentences.

1 Of course you can try to get a refund   A and decided just to do an interview.
2 I know the future looks depressing right now   B but I think you're flogging a dead horse.
3 They put the photo-story on hold for a while   C and I felt that I was going round in circles.
4 Everyone gave the same answers   D but nobody I know supports him.
5 A lot of exciting things are in the pipeline   E but there's always light at the end of the tunnel.
6 The polls indicate that our man is making headway   F but the details are all confidential at this stage.

Exercise 4

Choose the best answer to complete the sentences.

1 It appears that the police are beginning to _____ in the investigation.

   a get to grips   b bark up the wrong tree   c make headway

2 We had to put our lives _____ until we were both healthy again.

   a on hold   b in the doldrums   c on a roll

3 As these new ideas _____ attitudes started to change.

   a went round in circles b got on a roll   c gained ground

4 I wish you would stop wasting time and _____.

   a lose ground   b get your act together   c go round in circles

5 Your book needs a bit of editing but I think you're _____.

   a on the right track   b in the pipeline   c barking up the wrong tree

6 We are genuinely looking forward to the changes that are _____.

   a in the pipeline   b getting to grips   c going round in circles

Exercise 5

Replace the <u>underlined</u> words in sentences 1–8 with idioms A–H.

1 We may as well stop trying to achieve victory on this issue – we're just <u>wasting time</u>.

2 You need to <u>organize yourself</u> and start studying for your final exams.

3 It's been a difficult project but I feel that we are <u>progressing</u>, at last.

4 I'm afraid plans for an extension have to be <u>postponed</u> until we have enough money.

5 Things are still financially difficult for the company but we can <u>see the possibility of success</u>, at least.

6 Plans for a new tourist information office are <u>in development</u>, as well as a new shopping centre.

7 The detectives admit that they've been <u>following the wrong tree</u> for some time.

8 The industry has been <u>suffering a period of inactivity</u> with sales down 15 per cent on last year.

A in the pipeline

B in the doldrums

C barking up the wrong tree

D flogging a dead horse

E see light at the end of the tunnel

F get your act together

G put on hold

H making headway

Exercise 6

Correct the idioms in these sentences.

1 We have taken action to put the industry back on the right side of the track.

2 There are nearly 350 new hospital schemes going through the pipeline.

3 People feel hopeless. They don't see any light at the end of the pipeline.

4 The decision to buy the car was on a roll until we could sell our old one.

5 This new evidence suggests that we may be barking up a dead tree.

6 As a company, we are trying hard to put our act together on customer service.

7 Many of these firms are losing grips to new web-based businesses.

8 I was busy trying to get to hold with the new database.

Your turn!

Have you made any progress in your life or your work recently? Use the idioms in this unit to describe any of your experiences. For example:

I finally got to grips with uploading music to my phone.

I'm making headway with idioms and usually manage to use one every day.

His friends felt he wasn't really getting to grips with flying.

Expectation

the calm before the storm or the lull before the storm

You describe a very quiet period as the calm before the storm or the lull before the storm if it is followed by a period of trouble or intense activity.

Things are relatively relaxed at the moment but I think it's probably the calm before the storm.

The Emergency Department is fairly quiet, it's probably the lull before the storm.

castles in the air

If you describe someone's plans as castles in the air, you mean that they are not realistic and have no chance of succeeding.

The population began to understand that the president's election promises had been castles in the air.

not count your chickens or not count your chickens before they're hatched

If you say that you are not counting your chickens (before they're hatched), you mean that you are not making plans for the future because you do not know for certain how a particular situation will develop.

If we get through to the next stage we'll be competing against some top-class sides, so I'm not counting my chickens.

When dealing with important financial arrangements, never count your chickens before they're hatched.

NOTE   You can also use the proverb don't count your chickens before they're hatched from which this expression comes.

The contract is not signed yet. Don't count your chickens before they're hatched.

feel something in your bones

If you say that you can feel something in your bones, you mean that you feel very strongly that you are right about something, although you cannot explain why.

Joe, I have a hunch you're going to lose tonight. I just feel it in my bones.

NOTE   You can also use know, believe, and sense instead of feel.

Tradition is very important – you'd think a conservative would know that in his bones.

NOTE   You can also say that you have a feeling in your bones.

I've got a feeling in my bones we're going to lose this by-election.

not have a prayer

If you say that someone does not have a prayer, you mean that it is impossible for them to achieve something.

The team was on such good form their opponents didn't have a prayer.

it's early days or it's early in the day

If you say that it's early days or it's early in the day, you mean that it is too soon to be sure about what will happen about a situation in the future. [BRITISH]

We haven't made a lot of progress, but it's early days yet.

The spokesman did not expect any immediate changes. 'It is very early in the day yet.'

like looking for a needle in a haystack

If trying to find something is like looking for a needle in a haystack, it is extremely difficult or impossible.

She was told by police that searching for the dog would be like looking for a needle in a haystack.

NOTE   This usage of this expression is very variable.

It soon became clear that we were looking for a needle in a haystack.

It's very much a needle in a haystack situation *that we're dealing with.*

a long shot

If you describe a way of solving a problem as a long shot, you mean there is little chance that it will succeed but you think it worth trying.

NOTE   The reference here is to someone shooting at a target from a very long distance.

You could try to find her. It's a long shot *but you could start with her old school.*

on the cards

If something is on the cards, it is very likely to happen. [BRITISH]

NOTE   This is a reference to Tarot cards or other cards used to predict the future.

A major change in the way hospitals and schools are funded is on the cards.

on the off-chance

If you do something on the off-chance, you do it because there is a small chance that a good thing will happen even though you do not really expect it to. [mainly BRITISH]

She had turned up on the off-chance *of catching a glimpse of the princess.*

out of the blue

If something happens out of the blue it happens unexpectedly.

NOTE   This expression compares an unexpected event to a bolt of lightning from a blue sky.

Then, out of the blue *a solicitor's letter arrived.*

par for the course

If something that happens is par for the course, it is not good but it is what you expect.

NOTE   In golf, 'par' is the number of strokes a good golfer is expected to take for a particular hole or for the whole course.

There are leaves and branches all over the streets, and the power is out. But that's all par for the course *in a hurricane.*

not a snowball's chance in hell

If there is not a snowball's chance in hell of someone doing something or of something happening, there is no chance at all that they will do it or it will happen. [BRITISH, SPOKEN]

Do you seriously think he has a snowball's chance in hell *of winning this election?*

NOTE   You can also say that someone does not have a chance in hell of doing something.

They don't have a chance in hell *of privatizing the economy. They have no idea how a free market works.*

Exercise 1

Decide if the sentences are true (*T*) or false (*F*).

1 If there is calm before the storm, there will be a quiet period before a period of intense activity. ☐
2 If something comes out of the blue, it doesn't surprise you. ☐
3 If something is par for the course, it's better than expected. ☐
4 If something is a long shot, you don't expect it to be successful. ☐
5 If you do not count your chickens before they're hatched, you don't make plans for the future. ☐
6 If you feel something in your bones, you feel strongly that you are right about something. ☐

Exercise 2

Choose the best answer to complete the sentences.

1 They offered me the job right out of the _____.
  a blue   b storm   c sky

2 He's desperate to get the lead part in the play but he doesn't have a _____.
  a shot   b off-chance   c prayer

3 It's _____ days but the project appears to be developing well.
  a calm   b early   c blue

4 I called on the _____ -chance and happened to find her at home.
  a off   b on   c long

5 The classroom was horribly quiet but it was just the lull before the _____.
  a prayer   b storm   c coursev

6 I knew it was a long _____ but I thought I'd ask for a replacement anyway.
  a chance   b prayer   c shot

Exercise 3

Complete the sentences with the words in the box.

on	in	in	on	before	in	for	in

1 A good fisherman knows _____ his bones when it's going to rain.
2 Wearing black is par _____ the course at a formal event like this.
3 I phoned _____ the off-chance that you might like to join us.
4 History has shown that their dreams were just castles _____ the air.
5 None of us have a chance _____ hell of winning the lottery.
6 It's _____ the cards that he'll be the next prime minister.
7 The peace in the garden was the calm _____ the storm.
8 It's too early _____ the day to say if this is a good policy.

Exercise 4

Match idioms 1–6 with situations A–F.

1 Tom wants to pass his driving test before buying a car.

A He has a feeling in his bones.

2 The manager thinks the staff are unhappy about something.

B He's not counting his chickens.

3 Business has been good so we should make a profit this year.

C He doesn't have a chance in hell.

4 He suffered a knee injury – as so many tennis players do.

D It's on the cards.

5 You can't remember where you parked your car at the airport.

E It's like looking for a needle in a haystack.

6 Arif has entered a golf tournament even though he's never played before.

F That's par for the course.

Exercise 5

Re-order the phrases to make sentences. Add punctuation where necessary.

1 you shouldn't look / as it's been on the cards / for a long time / so surprised
2 to have a prayer / he did not seem / the world title / of regaining
3 for doctors who / par for the course / long hours are / are still training
4 by phoning the embassy / trying to find you / I admit that / was a bit of a long shot
5 more helpers / on the off-chance / I went / that they would need
6 which side / it's too early in the day / will win the match / to predict
7 building / the afternoon / they spent / castles in the air
8 in my bones / will be fine / that everything / I sense

Exercise 6

Match the <u>underlined</u> words and phrases in sentences 1–8 with an idiom with the same meaning A–H.

1 A new hospital is <u>likely to happen</u>, and so is a children's clinic.
2 It's still <u>only the beginning</u>, so it's difficult to say whether the business will be successful or not.
3 I need to locate a specific document in this pile of papers. It's <u>extremely difficult to find</u>.
4 I know you probably can't help me but I thought I'd ask <u>just in case there's a possibility</u>.
5 I'm sure he's going to propose to her – I <u>am convinced</u>!
6 He hasn't got <u>any possibility</u> of succeeding.
7 I think their order will be for 200 boxes but I don't want to <u>change our plans until that's confirmed</u>.
8 The report described our plans as <u>unrealistic and ambitious</u>.

A castles in the air
B a snowball's chance in hell
C like looking for a needle in a haystack
D feel it in my bones
E early days
F on the cards
G on the off-chance
H count our chickens before they're hatched

Your turn!

Use the idioms in this unit to describe any of your present or past expectations. For example:

I called round to see Jan on the off-chance yesterday.

It's early days to say whether I'll apply to study for a postgraduate degree.

Eddie **didn't have a snowball's chance in hell** of winning the world title.

Trouble and difficulty

be asking for trouble

If someone is asking for trouble, they are behaving in a way that makes it very likely that they will have problems.

Riding a bicycle in town after dark without lights is just asking for trouble.

bite off more than you can chew

If you bite off more than you can chew, you try to do a task that is too big for you or too difficult.

I didn't know if I could memorize a text of that length and started to worry that I had bitten off more than I could chew.

a Catch 22

A Catch 22 is an extremely frustrating situation in which one thing cannot happen until another thing has happened, but the other thing cannot happen until the first thing has happened.

NOTE This expression comes from the novel *Catch 22* (1961), by the American author Joseph Heller, which is about bomber pilots in the Second World War. Their 'Catch 22' situation was that any sane person would ask if they could stop flying. However, the authorities would only allow people to stop flying if they were insane.

There's a Catch 22 in finding a job. You need experience to get work and you need work to get experience.

NOTE You can also talk about a Catch 22 situation.

It's a Catch 22 situation here. Nobody wants to support you until you're successful but without the support, how can you ever be successful?

a/the fly in the ointment

If someone or something is a fly in the ointment they prevent a situation from being as successful or happy as it would be without them.

NOTE Ointment is a creamy medicinal substance for treating pain or wounds.

The only fly in the ointment is Bella's lack of concentration.

not have a leg to stand on

If someone does not have a leg to stand on they are in a very weak position, because they cannot prove a claim or statement they have made.

You'd never win if you went to court. Our lawyers said you wouldn't have a leg to stand on.

in over your head

If you are in over your head you are in a situation that is too difficult for you to deal with.

NOTE Here, the reference is to getting into water that is too deep to stand up in.

He realized that he was in over his head, and that only his family could help him.

NOTE You can also say that someone gets in over their head if they get into a situation that is too difficult for them.

Kelly told the hearing he got in way over his head and became afraid after the prisoner threatened him and his family.

out of the frying pan into the fire or from the frying pan into the fire

If someone has gone out of the frying pan into the fire or from the frying pan into the fire, they have moved from a bad situation to an even worse one.

I was hoping to get my career back on track after a bad time, but as it turned out, I'd gone out of the frying pan into the fire.

an own goal

An own goal is a course of action which is intended to bring you an advantage and which instead causes a problem for you. [BRITISH]

NOTE   In sports such as football and hockey if someone scores an own goal, they accidentally score a goal for the team they are playing against by knocking the ball into their own net.

It was a classic own goal by the fashion house. They brought their prices down to attract more customers but lost the high-end customers that they already had.

put your foot in it

If you put your foot in it you say something which embarrasses or offends the person you are with, and embarrasses you as a result.

I put my foot in it straight away, referring to folk music. Tom sat forward and glared. 'It's not folk music, man. It's heritage music.'

a stumbling block

If you describe something as a stumbling block you mean it is a problem which stops you from achieving something.

It's her attitude that's the biggest stumbling block.

teething problems or teething troubles

Teething problems or teething troubles are problems in the early stages of something. [BRITISH]

NOTE   When babies are teething their teeth are starting to appear through their gums, often causing them pain.

There are bound to be teething problems in a new marriage.

Some teething troubles aside, the new computer system works well.

a vicious circle

If you describe a difficult situation as a vicious circle you mean that one problem has caused other problems which, in turn, have made the original problem even worse.

NOTE   It is impossible to prove the truth of one statement by a second statement, which in turn relies on the first for proof. The expression is a translation of the Latin 'circulus vitiosus', meaning 'a flawed circular argument'.

The economy couldn't create jobs because consumers weren't spending. Consumers weren't spending because the economy wasn't creating jobs. And this was the vicious circle we were caught in.

Exercise 1

Complete the sentences with the words in the box.

| fly | block | circle | trouble | goal | leg | foot | head |

1 He put his _____ in it by asking if she was going to marry Craig.
2 I'm in over my _____ with debt just now.
3 The cost of the solution is the biggest stumbling _____.
4 I haven't got a _____ to stand on because I have no witnesses.
5 So often with many health problems, a vicious _____ is established.
6 The suspect scored an own _____ by making a phone call that the police recorded.
7 If you post that picture on the Internet you're asking for _____.
8 The _____ in the ointment was that the sound system was not powerful enough.

Exercise 2

Answer the questions.

1 Does a fly in the ointment lead to or prevent a successful outcome?
2 Is a stumbling block something that stops or helps you from reaching your goals?
3 Are teething troubles temporary or permanent problems?
4 If you are in something over your head, are you able or unable to cope with a situation?
5 Is a person usually pleased or offended if you put your foot in it when you say something to them?
6 Does a vicious circle usually have a definite good outcome or not?

Exercise 3

Complete the sentences. Choose the correct idioms.

1 I really don't think you should attempt all that in one day. *You're putting your foot in it. / It's biting off more than you can chew. / It's a stumbling block*.
2 I'm sure things will improve. Everyone has *a fly in the ointment / a vicious circle / teething problems* when they first start a new job.
3 I can't get a teaching job without a qualification and I can't get a qualification without some teaching experience. It's *a Catch 22 situation. / a stumbling block. / an own goal*.
4 I really *didn't have a leg to stand on / put my foot in it / was in over my head* when I asked her how her husband was. I didn't realise they'd separated.
5 I wouldn't leave one bad situation to go into another, even worse one. It'll be *a fly in the ointment. / putting your foot in it. / going from the frying pan into the fire*.
6 The only *stumbling block / vicious circle / teething troubles* to my chances of getting a promotion is my lack of experience in the field.

Exercise 4

Correct the idioms in these sentences.

1 I found myself in a ridiculous Circle 22 situation.
2 It's a vicious round because the fear gets worse each time she sees a cat, and now she's afraid of the fear itself.
3 This job is really too difficult for us now – we're in up to our legs.
4 I scored my own goal when I told my boss I didn't really need a pay rise.
5 The block in the ointment is the fact that you really need a fast broadband Internet connection to play these games properly.
6 You might have bitten off more trouble than you can chew with this project.
7 Restaurants inevitably suffer tooth troubles when they are establishing themselves.
8 Letting a child near a can of spray paint is just asking for troubles.

Exercise 5

Complete the sentences with idioms from this unit, changing the verb forms if necessary.

1 A politician can score _____ if a publicity photo makes him look ridiculous.
2 After some initial _____, the business began to do well.
3 Having finally left one bad relationship, she jumped _____.
4 You don't have a formal contract with the company so I'm afraid you haven't really got _____.
5 Leaving valuable possessions in a car is asking _____.
6 Here is a ten-point guide to help you avoid putting _____ when you meet your girlfriend's father.

Exercise 6

Complete the table. Put the idioms in the correct groups.

a stumbling block | a Catch 22 | a vicious circle | the fly in the ointment | an own goal
bite off more than you can chew | put your foot in it | in over your head | not have a leg to stand on
out of the frying pan into the fire

causing difficulty	1 _____
	2 _____
	3 _____
	4 _____
	5 _____
a difficult situation	1 _____
	2 _____
	3 _____
	4 _____
	5 _____

Your turn!

Use the idioms in this unit to describe any troublesome or difficult situations you have experienced recently. For example:

It's great that we have a day off next week. The fly in the ointment is that I'll have to revise for my exam the next day.

My friend Jose is always putting his foot in it but he's a really nice person.

WORLD WEIGHTLIFTING RECORD ATTEMPT

His friends had said he was **in over his head**, but he decided to persevere.

Safety and risk

by the skin of your teeth

If you do something by the skin of your teeth you just manage to do it but very nearly fail.

In the men's First Division, the champions survived by the skin of their teeth.

a close shave

If someone has a close shave they very nearly have a bad accident or very nearly suffer a defeat.

NOTE   This is a reference to shaving with a dangerously sharp razor.

McGregor had a close shave when a seven foot polar bear ran at him while he was filming a documentary about the animals in Canada.

the coast is clear

If the coast is clear you are able to do something because nobody is there to see you doing it.

NOTE   This expression may refer to smugglers (= people who take things illegally into a country) sending messages that there were no coastguards near and it was safe to land or set sail.

'You can come out now,' he called. 'The coast is clear. She's gone!'

a good bet or a safe bet

If something is a good bet or a safe bet it is a sensible or useful thing to do or use.

If you want something smart to wear to a friend's wedding, a dark suit is a good bet.

NOTE   You can also say that something would be a better bet or a safer bet, meaning that it would be more sensible or useful than another possibility.

I was going to buy an apartment but I'm now thinking a house might be a better bet.

NOTE   You can also say that something is someone's best bet or safest bet, meaning that it is the most sensible or useful thing to do.

If you really want to keep your home safe from robbery, your best bet is still to buy a dog.

in safe hands

If someone or something is in safe hands they are being looked after by someone who will make sure they are not harmed or damaged.

They could get on with their own lives, knowing their girls were in safe hands.

NOTE   You can sometimes use other adjectives instead of safe.

Although I knew the children would be in good hands, I still felt anxious.

He was forced to give up his business, which is now in the capable hands of his only son.

play it safe

If you play safe or play it safe, you do not take any risks.

If you want to play safe, cut down on the amount of salt you eat.

The pilot decided that Christchurch was too far away and played it safe, landing at Wellington.

be playing with fire

If you are playing with fire you are doing something that has big risks and is likely to cause problems.

In this economic climate, union leaders who are thinking about strikes are playing with fire.

put all your eggs in one basket

If you put all your eggs in one basket you put all your efforts or resources into one course of action and will not be able to do anything else if this fails.

You could argue this is a risky strategy, putting all your eggs in one basket; if the firm goes bust you lose your job and your savings and everything.

NOTE   People sometimes put other words before eggs and basket to show a particular situation they are talking about.

Never put all your investment eggs in one basket.

These countries have put their development eggs in the tourism basket, spending millions of dollars from public funds to build the sorts of facilities that foreign tourists demand.

be skating on thin ice

If someone is skating on thin ice they are doing something which could have unpleasant consequences for them.

He told me I was skating on thin ice and should change my attitude.

NOTE   You can use verbs such as tread, walk, or stand instead of skate.

'Watch it Max,' Christopher thought to himself, 'you're treading on very thin ice.'

NOTE   You can also just say that someone is on thin ice.

I could see I was on thin ice. We'd had similar pointless arguments many times before.

stick your neck out

If you stick your neck out, you say something which other people are afraid to say, even though this may cause trouble for you.

NOTE   This expression may come from boxing, where fighters need to keep their necks and chins drawn in or protected in order to avoid being hit by their opponent.

At the risk of sticking my neck out, I doubt whether the attempt will be successful.

take your life in your hands or take your life into your hands

If you take your life in your hands or take your life into your hands when you do something, you take a lot of risks when you do it.

A rider who does not know the road takes his life in his hands by cycling in the dark.

You take your life into your hands just crossing the road in this city.

to be on the safe side

If you do something to be on the safe side you do it to protect yourself from harm or trouble, although it is unlikely to be necessary.

I didn't think it was serious but I took her to the doctor's just to be on the safe side.

Exercise 1

Match idioms A–F with situations 1–3.

1 taking a risk   ☐ ☐
2 only just avoiding danger or disappointment   ☐ ☐
3 being sure to avoid danger or disappointment   ☐ ☐

A It's best to be on the safe side and take more money than you think you'll really need.
B The vehicles just touched as they passed each other so it was a close shave.
C You take your life in your hands when you accept a lift from Jo!
D We've decided to play it safe and book a coach for 40 even though we're really only expecting 30 students.
E You are playing with fire if you deal with these so-called 'protection agents'.
F The train was just about to leave so I ran like mad and caught it by the skin of my teeth.

Exercise 2

Match sentence halves 1–6 with A–F to make complete sentences.

1 You're playing with fire if you do that.
2 You can come out of your hiding place.
3 I'd go to the doctor about that rash,
4 She's a very experienced babysitter –
5 You passed by the skin of your teeth –
6 I'm not going to stick my neck out

A your children will be in safe hands, don't worry.
B just to be on the safe side.
C The coast is clear.
D Why do you want to take such a risk?
E for someone who never takes a risk for me.
F you might not be so lucky next time.

Exercise 3

Choose the best answer to complete the sentences.

1 I know I'm _____ but I have to say that I don't agree with any of you about this.

   a sticking my neck out
   b sticking my life into my hands
   c sticking all my eggs in one basket

2 They had left their child with their close friends so they knew she was _____.

   a on the safe side
   b a safe bet
   c in safe hands

3 The management is under a lot of financial pressure so you will be _____ if you ask for a pay rise now.

   a playing it safe
   b putting all your eggs in one basket
   c skating on thin ice

4 They expect to sell all this stock by the end of the year, which is _____ as business has been very good so far.

   a a close shave
   b a safe bet
   c by the skin of their teeth

5 When she was sure _____, she opened the letter.

   a the coast was clear
   b it was a close shave
   c she was skating on thin ice

6 That road is so dangerous that every time you cross it, you _____.

   a are skating on thin ice
   b take your life in your hands
   c put all your eggs in one basket

Exercise 4

Match situations 1–6 with sentences A–F with the same meaning.

1 You nearly missed your usual bus.
2 You decided not to specialize in just one subject yet.
3 You always carry an umbrella in your bag, even in summer.
4 You want to avoid your classmates.
5 You agree to do whatever the rest of the group wants to do.
6 You arrive late for a class with a very strict teacher.

A You don't want to stick your neck out.
B You are treading on thin ice.
C You wait to get coffee until the coast is clear.
D You got it by the skin of your teeth.
E You prefer to play it safe.
F You don't want to put all your eggs in one basket.

Exercise 5

Complete the sentences with idioms from this unit.

1 The export business is risky; if you try it you'll be playing with _____.
2 I know you are an expert and I'm in safe _____.
3 The horse riders will be out in the park soon but for now the coast is _____.
4 She was there when the fighting started and escaped by the skin of her _____.
5 I managed to avoid that awful Mrs. Lee in the supermarket but it was a close _____.
6 Let's allow ourselves a bit more time than we'll probably need, to be on the safe _____.
7 They bought their tickets online in advance because they thought that was the safest _____.
8 Study hard at school and always keep an alternative job in mind – to avoid putting your eggs in one _____.

Exercise 6

Correct the idioms in these sentences.

1 It's not a good idea to put all your life in one basket.
2 She never sticks her hands out, even when she feels strongly that she should say something about a bad situation.
3 Be careful. You're standing on thin ice by being so direct with your boss.
4 Phew! Coming face to face with that terrifying dog was a clean shave!
5 The shed is quite hazardous, full of sharp tools and dangerous objects. You take your head in your hands when you go in there.
6 You can get to the resort by coach, train or car, but if you want a quick journey, the plane is probably the best coast.
7 He was playing with life by driving the car after it had been in the crash.
8 It seemed like a good shave that the traffic warden wouldn't come soon.

Your turn!

Use the idioms in this unit to talk about safety and/or risk in your life. For example:

I like to play it safe and take an umbrella with me when I go out.

I'm learning English at a good university so I know I'm in safe hands.

She avoided a catastrophe by **the skin of her teeth.**

20

Money

cost an arm and a leg

If something costs an arm and a leg it costs a lot of money.

It cost us an arm and a leg to get here. But it has been worth every penny and more.

NOTE   You can use verbs such as pay, charge, and spend instead of cost.

Many restaurants were charging an arm and a leg for poor quality food.

down the drain

If money, work, or time has gone down the drain it has been lost or wasted.

Over the years, the government has poured billions of dollars down the drain supporting its national airlines and other firms.

You have ruined everything – my perfect plans, my great organization. All those years of work are down the drain.

NOTE   You can sometimes use words such as plughole and toilet instead of drain.

Millions of dollars have gone down the plughole.

feel the pinch

If a person or organization feels the pinch they do not have as much money as they used to have, and so they cannot buy the things they would like to buy.

Poor households were still feeling the pinch and new taxes on fuel made matters even worse.

have deep pockets

If a person or organization has deep pockets they have a lot of money.

The company will do anything to avoid scandal – and everyone knows it has deep pockets.

NOTE   You can also talk about people or organizations with deep pockets or use deep pockets on its own with the same meaning.

They needed to find investors with deep pockets. What they lacked in military power, they made up for in deep pockets.

in the red

If a person or organization is in the red they owe money to someone or to another organization.

NOTE   This expression comes from the practice in the past of using red ink to fill in entries on the debit side of a book of accounts.

Banks are desperate for you to join them – even if you're in the red.

NOTE   You can also say that you go into the red when you start to owe money to the bank.

If you do go into the red, you get charged 30 pence for each transaction while you are overdrawn.

NOTE   You can also say that a person or organization gets out of the red, meaning that they stop owing money to someone.

We're slowly climbing out of the red.

NOTE   You can use in the black to talk about being in credit.

My bank account was in the black for the first time that year.

make ends meet

If you find it difficult to make ends meet you find it difficult to pay for the things you need in life, because you have very little money.

> NOTE Originally, this expression was 'make both ends of the year meet', which meant to spend only as much money as you received as income.

Many people are struggling to make ends meet because wages are failing to keep pace with rising prices.

on a shoestring

If you do something on a shoestring, you do it using very little money.

> NOTE In American English, shoelaces are called shoestrings. The reference here is to the very small amount of money that is needed to buy shoelaces.

This theatre was always run on a shoestring.

> NOTE You can use shoestring before a noun.

Both films were made on a shoestring budget.

out of pocket

If you are out of pocket after an event or an activity, you have less money than you should have.

The promoter claims he was left £36,000 out of pocket after the concert.

be rolling in it or be rolling in money

If someone is rolling in it or is rolling in money, they are very rich. [INFORMAL]

Don't worry about the cost – soon you'll be rolling in it.

Jessica's parents are obviously rolling in money.

a small fortune

A small fortune is a very large amount of money.

For almost two years, Hawkins made a small fortune running a corner shop.

there's no such thing as a free lunch or there is no free lunch

People say there's no such thing as a free lunch or there is no free lunch to mean you cannot expect to get things for nothing.

> NOTE This expression dates back to at least 1840 in the United States. It recently became popular again when the American economist Milton Friedman used it in the 1970s.

There is no such thing as a free lunch of course, and many of the most attractive looking deals have quite large joining fees.

There is no free lunch. You won't get anything you don't sweat and struggle for.

tighten your belt

If you tighten your belt you make an effort to spend less money.

Clearly, if you are spending more than your income, you'll need to tighten your belt.

Exercise 1

Match idioms A–F with situations 1–3.

1 having a lot of money   ☐ ☐
2 having no money   ☐ ☐
3 very expensive   ☐ ☐

A With the rising prices of food and petrol, we all have to tighten our belts these days.
B He's got a good job and has inherited money from his family, so he's rolling in it.
C It'll cost an arm and a leg to travel there by train.
D I've just been paid, and already I'm in the red.
E I'm sure Matthew will lend you the money – he seems to have very deep pockets.
F That trip must have cost them a small fortune.

Exercise 2

Choose the best answer to complete the sentences.

1 I don't earn much so it's not always easy to make _____ meet.
    a pockets   b ends   c your belt

2 That meal we had in the hotel restaurant was superb, but it cost _____.
    a an arm and a leg   b deep pockets   c the pinch

3 You should do your best not to let your account go into the _____, or you might get fined by your bank.
    a red   b ends   c black

4 They have just received a pay rise. The company they work for has _____.
    a an arm and a leg   b to make ends meet   c deep pockets

5 We'll be travelling _____ as the exchange rate is very bad for us just now.
    a on a shoestring   b out of pocket   c in the red

6 Have you seen the size of their house? They must be _____ in it.
    a making   b rolling   c draining

Exercise 3

Match sentence halves 1–6 with A–F to make complete sentences.

1 I've lost all the money I invested in that company.
2 They've both lost their jobs so
3 We had hardly any money but we managed to travel around
4 You should have expected the hidden charges.
5 Some of the insurance companies have deep pockets –
6 We're all feeling the pinch

A it's a struggle to make ends meet.
B now that the economy is in recession.
C why don't you approach them for sponsorship?
D It was just money down the drain.
E There's no such thing as a free lunch after all!
F on a shoestring.

Exercise 4

Read the statements and answer the questions.

1 She had to learn to tighten her belt when she became a student.
    Did she have more or less money before she was a student?

2 They're feeling the pinch more now because they've moved to the city.
    Do they find it cheaper or more expensive to live in the city?

3 Laura said 'I'll give you the money for my theatre ticket tomorrow David. I don't want you to be out of pocket.'
    Who paid for the tickets at the theatre?

4 They'll give us sandwiches and coffee at the meeting but we know there's no such thing as a free lunch.
    Do they have to buy their sandwiches and coffee?

5 Stefan's piano lessons are just money down the plughole!
    Is Stefan doing well at learning to play the piano?

6 We are really careful about how much electricity we use in order to make ends meet.
    Do they find it difficult to pay for their electricity?

Exercise 5

Re-order the phrases to make sentences. Add punctuation where necessary.

1 he should not / he was paid / in advance so / be out of pocket
2 so from now on / he has just lost his job / he will have trouble / making ends meet
3 a swimming pool / be rolling in money / in the garden must / a family who have
4 a small fortune / to take the whole group / it will cost / on a foreign tour
5 it seems to me that / to get around is / money down the drain / paying for taxis
6 has deep pockets and / the organization / to pay well / can afford
7 for tickets / to pay an arm and a leg / to the cup final / we had
8 and even / out of the red / the company / make a profit / hopes to climb

Exercise 6

Choose the most appropriate thing to say A–F in each situation 1–6.

1 We're wasting a lot of money on this project.
2 We can't expect to get something for nothing.
3 We all have to try and spend less money for a while.
4 We can afford to buy it – we've got lots of money.
5 We haven't paid back the money the bank lent us yet.
6 We'll have to try and complete the project as cheaply as possible.

A We've got deep pockets.
B We're pouring money down the drain.
C We're still in the red.
D We need to do it on a shoestring budget.
E We need to tighten our belts.
F There's no such thing as a free lunch.

Exercise 7

Correct the idioms in these sentences.

1 Worsening economic problems mean that ordinary voters are beginning to feel the pinching.
2 The senator says he will continue his on a shoestring campaign in every part of the state.
3 The company was already in the red side, owing more than three million pounds.
4 Freda didn't know much about antiques but she was sure the table was worth a deep fortune.
5 They seem to think they can charge a leg and a foot for their services because we all need them.
6 Business organizations across the land are making up their belts and trying to cut costs.
7 If we don't have results soon, we'll be accused of throwing money into the plughole.
8 You seem to think that all doctors are lying in money!

Your turn!

Have you had to think about money recently? Use the idioms in this unit to describe your experiences.
For example:

I've been feeling the pinch since I was a student.

It costs an arm and a leg to pay for a Master's degree.

Like most students, Tom had to live **on a shoestring**.

Authority and control

be breathing down someone's neck

If someone is breathing down your neck they are closely watching and checking everything that you do.

Most farmers have bank managers breathing down their necks, so have to give an economic reason for everything they do.

call the shots

If you call the shots you are the person who makes all the important decisions in an organization or situation. [INFORMAL]

> NOTE   This may refer to someone shooting and saying which part of the target they intend to hit. Alternatively, it may refer to a snooker or pool player saying which ball they intend to hit or which pocket they intend to hit it into.

Is the military really the power behind the President now? Who really calls the shots?

get out of hand

If a situation gets out of hand it cannot be controlled any longer.

The two men had an argument that got out of hand and the police were called.

go over someone's head

If you go over the head of someone in authority you communicate directly with someone in a higher position to try to get what you want.

He was criticized for trying to go over the heads of senior officers.

have someone eating out of your hand or have someone eating out of the palm of your hand

If you have someone eating out of your hand or have them eating out of the palm of your hand, they will do whatever you want because they like or admire you so much.

> NOTE   The image here is of a wild animal that is tame enough to take food from a person's hand.

No one can handle reporters like she can. She usually has them eating out of her hand by the time they leave.

in high places

People in high places are people who have power and influence in a group or society.

You do not succeed so quickly without having a few friends in high places.

a law unto yourself

If you describe a person or organization as a law unto themselves, you mean that they do what they want, ignoring laws, rules, or usual ways of doing things.

He does his work well but in his own way. He is truly a law unto himself.

on top of something

If you are on top of a task or situation you are dealing with it successfully.

The government does not seem on top of the situation.

NOTE   If you are beginning to deal with a task or situation successfully, you can say that you are getting on top of it.

We are getting on top of crime but there is still a lot to be done.

pass the buck

If you accuse someone of passing the buck you are accusing them of failing to take responsibility for a problem and of expecting someone else to deal with it instead.

His three commanders-in-chief were arguing and passing the buck to one another.

pull strings

If someone pulls strings to get something they want they get it by using their friendships with powerful people, often in a way which is unfair.

They felt that her father was pulling strings to advance her career.

put your foot down

If you put your foot down you tell someone forcefully that they must do something or that they must not do something.

Annabel went through a phase of saying: 'I can do my homework and watch TV at the same time'. Naturally I put my foot down.

twist someone around your little finger or wrap someone around your little finger

If you can twist someone around your little finger or wrap them around your little finger you can make them do anything you want them to.

Anna may not be the brightest person in the world but she knew exactly how to twist him around her little finger.

NOTE   You can use wind instead of twist or wrap and round instead of around.

I didn't think there was a man in the world you were afraid of Christabel, or one you couldn't wind round your finger.

twist someone's arm

If you twist someone's arm you try hard to persuade them to do something.

I had to twist their arms to get them to start working with me but once they did, it went well.

wear the trousers or wear the pants

If one person in a couple wears the trousers [BRITISH] or wears the pants [AMERICAN] they make all the important decisions.

NOTE   This expression is usually used about women who seem to control their husbands or partners.

She may give the impression that she wears the trousers but it's actually Tim who makes all the big decisions.

My father said he wanted to discuss the investment with my mother, to which the salesman demanded, 'Who wears the pants in your family?'

Exercise 1

Complete the sentences with the words in the box.

neck | hand | finger | arm | foot | finger | head | hand

1 If you won't allow it I shall simply go over your _____ and speak to your manager.
2 I can't work with you breathing down my _____ all the time.
3 He is a very clever lawyer, famous for always having the jury eating out of the palm of his _____.
4 She's always been able to wrap her grandfather around her little _____.
5 I wish the teacher would put her _____ down and stop the children chatting so much.
6 The company is losing money fast and the situation is getting out of _____.
7 If you twist his _____ hard enough he'll probably see that you're right.
8 That child will try to wind you round his _____ if he possibly can.

Exercise 2

Decide if the sentences are true (*T*) or false (*F*).

1 People in high places are important people. ☐
2 Someone who is a law unto themselves does things the same way as everyone else. ☐
3 If someone calls the shots they follow someone else's orders. ☐
4 If someone twists your arm they persuade you to do something. ☐
5 If someone is on top of something that person hasn't got things under control. ☐
6 If someone passes the buck that person takes responsibility for a task. ☐
7 A person who pulls strings manages to do something because of their connections with someone. ☐
8 If someone is breathing down your neck they are watching you closely. ☐

Exercise 3

Choose the best answer to complete the sentences.

1 You may be unhappy but you shouldn't _____ unless you feel your boss is being irresponsible.

  a eat out of his hand   b go over his head   c get out of hand

2 Many parents are tempted to _____ to schools and other organizations for teaching their children about moral issues.

  a pass the buck   b get out of hand   c go over their heads

3 We've had some serious problems but we think we're _____ now.

  a getting out of hand   b passing the buck   c getting on top of them

4 He likes to be in control of everything – he's always the one who _____.

  a gets out of hand   b calls the shots   c passes the buck

5 She knows a lot of people in the theatre so she's usually able to _____ to get the tickets she wants.

  a call the shots   b pass the buck   c pull strings

Exercise 4

Re-order the phrases to make sentences. Add punctuation where necessary.

1 when their children / try to / to teachers / pass the buck / misbehave / some parents
2 your son's behaviour / put your foot down / you / it's time / about
3 twisted around your little finger / he'll do anything / because / you ask / you've got him
4 get out of hand / stop the debate / things / if / I'll
5 other people / don't / call the shots / let / all the time
6 I'll see / pull any strings / an interview / if I can / to get you
7 has always been / the newspaper / a law unto himself / the editor of
8 his view / the people / did not share / in high places

Exercise 5

Complete the sentences with idioms from this unit, changing the verb forms if necessary. Some sentences can take more than one idiom.

1 It's not difficult to see who _____ in that relationship.
2 Most parents understand the need to calm situations like this before they _____.
3 No one's _____: you don't have to buy one or both – it's a free choice.
4 Predictably, customer services _____ back to Internet services who suggested I ring customer services.
5 We weren't getting anywhere with the district manager so we decided to _____.
6 Those children behave very badly – their father should _____.

Exercise 6

Complete the table. Put idioms in the correct groups.

breathing down someone's neck	twist/wrap someone around your little finger
wear the trousers	go over someone's head	call the shots	on top of something
have someone eating out of your hand	put your foot down	twist someone's arm	pull strings

being in control	1 _____
	2 _____
	3 _____
	4 _____
	5 _____
using influence	1 _____
	2 _____
	3 _____
	4 _____
	5 _____

Your turn!

Think about the people in your life who have authority or control. Use the idioms in this unit to describe any of your experiences with them. For example:

I've got my history teacher eating out of my hand *since I got full marks in the exam.*

I think I know who wears the trousers *in our house.*

Everyone knew she **wore the trousers** in their relationship.

Limitations and restrictions

bend the rules

If you bend the rules you do something which is not allowed, either to help someone else or for your own advantage.

I'm prepared to bend the rules – I may even have to break them.

NOTE You can also say that you stretch the rules.

He accused the company of stretching the sport's rules to the limit.

the dos and don'ts

The dos and don'ts of a particular situation are the things you should and should not do in that situation.

Disasters can be avoided if a few general dos and don'ts are considered.

draw the line

1 If someone knows where to draw the line they know at what point an activity or situation stops being reasonable and starts to be unacceptable.

It is difficult for charities to know where to draw the line between acceptable and unacceptable sources of finance.

2 If you draw the line at a particular activity you would not do it because you disapprove of it or because it is so extreme.

I'll do almost anything – although I think I'd draw the line at running naked across the stage!

NOTE There are several theories about the origin of this expression. It may come from early versions of tennis in which the court had no fixed size: players agreed their own limits and drew lines accordingly. Alternatively, it may be connected with the 16th century practice of using a plough to cut a line across a field to indicate a boundary between two plots of land. A third possibility is that it refers to boxing matches in the past, when a line was drawn in the ring which neither boxer could cross.

a fine line between something

If there is a fine line between two different activities or situations there is a point at which they are very similar, often when one activity or situation is acceptable and the other is not.

There is a fine line between being nicely looked after and never being left alone.

NOTE You can also talk about a thin line between two things or a narrow line between two things.

There is a thin line between being a good player and being one of the best.

There's a narrow line between being interested and being nosy.

have your hands full

If you have your hands full you are very busy.

NOTE You often use this expression to show that someone has many responsibilities or jobs and not enough time for any more.

She's doing fine. She's got her hands full with the kids of course.

NOTE You can also say that someone's hands are full.

He's managing all three projects so his hands are full.

off limits

1 If an area is off limits you are not allowed to go there.

The area was kept off limits to foreign journalists until early this year.

2 If something is off limits you are not allowed to have it or do it.

Of course, smoking was off limits everywhere.

out of bounds

If a place is out of bounds you are not allowed to go there.

The area has been out of bounds to foreigners for more than a month.

NOTE   You can use out-of-bounds before a noun.

Avoid signposted out-of-bounds areas.

over the top

If you describe something as over the top you think that it is too extreme.

NOTE   During the First World War 'to go over the top' meant to climb out of the trenches (=long, narrow channels in the ground) and run into no-man's land (=land that is not controlled by either side) in order to attack the enemy.

At one point, which I think is a bit over the top, he talks about the end of civilization.

NOTE   You can also say that someone goes over the top if they do something in a way that is too extreme.

Maybe he went a bit over the top with some of his language.

overstep the mark

If you overstep the mark you offend people by doing something that is considered to be rude or unacceptable.

NOTE   The 'mark' in this expression may be the line behind which runners stand before a race. Alternatively it may refer to boxing matches in the past, when a line was drawn in the ground which neither boxer could cross.

They agreed that by criticizing his manager so publicly, Taylor had overstepped the mark.

step on someone's toes or tread on someone's toes

If you step on someone's toes or tread on their toes you offend them by interfering in something that is their responsibility.

Small shopkeepers know who sells what so they don't step on one another's toes.

She's already seeing another doctor about this problem – I can't tread on his toes.

with no strings attached or without strings

If you say that an offer of help comes with no strings attached or without strings you mean that accepting the offer does not require you to do a particular thing or give something in return.

I think this is an extremely generous offer. There are no strings attached and I will recommend that everyone accepts.

We must reduce our dependence on government money, which never comes without strings.

your hands are tied

If your hands are tied something such as a law is preventing you from acting in the way that you want to.

He would like to help but his hands are tied by the regulations.

[note] You can also say that you have your hands tied or that something ties your hands.

The present rule ties jockeys' hands and I don't feel it is fair.

She felt frustrated by it all. 'We feel as though our hands have been tied because we have no power at all.'

Exercise 1

Choose the best answer to complete the sentences.

1 There's a fine _____ between fact and fantasy in this TV programme.

   a line   b mark   c limit

2 Ali realized that this time he'd probably overstepped the _____.

   a limit   b mark   c line

3 Perhaps I was a bit over the _____, accusing you of being a traitor.

   a line   b top   c mark

4 I asked if he's ever been tempted to bend the _____ for a good cause.

   a rules   b strings   c line

5 The site of the disaster is completely off _____ to reporters.

   a strings   b limits   c bounds

6 The editor allowed the photos to be taken but drew the _____ at publishing them.

   a bounds   b strings   c line

7 When she's not writing her hands are _____ with her family.

   a bound   b empty   c full

8 The spokesman said that his hands were _____ and he could not account for the delay.

   a fine   b tied   c bound

Exercise 2

Match sentence halves 1–6 with A–F to make complete sentences.

1 I'll make it clear that the kitchen

2 The college said the donation

3 I want to make some changes but with no budget –

4 The director asked me to make suggestions but

5 A poster on the kitchen wall

6 I didn't stop to talk because he obviously

A had his hands full.

B my hands are tied.

C I'm afraid of treading on his toes.

D had been made with no strings attached.

E shows all the important dos and don'ts.

F is completely out of bounds.

Exercise 3

Use sentences A–F to answer questions 1–6.

1 Who has gone a bit over the top?

2 Who has decided to draw the line?

3 Who's hands are full?

4 Who's hands are tied?

5 Who doesn't want to step on anyone's toes?

6 Who has decided to stretch the rules?

A Birgit's got two part-time jobs and four children.

B Roger has refused to accept any more invitations.

C Leo asked his colleague if he was already dealing with the matter.

D It's not usually allowed, but Atsuko has decided to let parents watch the class.

E Arif can't complete the order without his boss's permission.

F Jenny has told her teenage daughters they won't ever be allowed to go out in the evening again.

Exercise 4

Replace the underlined words with the idioms in the box.

> off limits | my hands are tied | step on someone's toes | I've got my hands full.
> overstepped the mark | dos and don'ts

1 I'm sorry I can't help you at the moment. I'm really busy.

2 It's a good idea to read the list of things you should and shouldn't do before you arrive.

3 I'd love to help but I'm afraid I am not allowed to.

4 I want to make sure I don't offend anyone by interfering with their responsibilities.

5 Going into the fields next to the school is not allowed. They are not accessible.

6 Please apologise. You've really done something unacceptable.

Exercise 5

Match situations 1–8 with idioms A–H.

1 We are not allowed to use the roof terrace at the top of the building.

2 I've been given an amazing opportunity without having to do anything in return.

3 I think going on holiday in a private jet was a bit extreme.

4 Swearing in the classroom is unacceptable. Don't do it again.

5 Sometimes you can do things that are theoretically not allowed.

6 How could you say such a mean and nasty thing? That's very rude of you.

7 I'm afraid I can't help you because you work for a different department.

8 I've got far too many other things to do just now.

A My hands are full.

B My hands are tied.

C It was over the top.

D I draw the line at it.

E You've overstepped the mark.

F It's out of bounds.

G There are no strings attached.

H You can bend the rules.

Exercise 6

Correct the idioms in these sentences.

1 There's a full line between bravery and foolishness.

2 When he occasionally overstepped the line he would immediately apologize.

3 There is no classical music which is out of limits for children, they say.

4 I am grateful to them for their co-operation, which was given with no lines attached.

5 The policy is flexible – staff waiting for an important call can bend the toes provided the phone remains on silent.

6 The publisher produces a booklet full of don'ts and dos for new authors.

7 The council says their toes are tied by government spending limits.

8 He was smart enough not to tread on his colleagues' lines.

Your turn!

Are there any limitations and restrictions in your life? Use the idioms in this unit to describe them.
For example:

I've got my hands full **with schoolwork at the moment.**

My friends went a bit over the top **inviting everyone they could think of to their party.**

There are certain do's and dont's to remember when you fill up your car with fuel.

Loving and liking

carry a torch for someone

If you carry a torch for someone, you are in love with them but they do not love you.

NOTE The torch referred to in these expressions is a long stick with burning material at one end which provides a light. This kind of torch is sometimes used in processions or parades.

What makes a woman so special that a man will carry a torch for her all his life?

NOTE You can use the verb hold instead of carry.

He never saw the woman again. And he went through the rest of his life holding a torch for her.

common-or-garden or garden-variety

You use common-or-garden [BRITISH] or garden-variety [AMERICAN] to describe something of a very ordinary kind, with no special features.

NOTE These expressions were originally used to describe the most ordinary variety of a species of plant.

These are designer rain boots – not your common-or-garden wellington boots.

The experiment itself is garden-variety science that normally would attract little public attention.

fall head over heels or fall head over heels in love

If you fall head over heels or fall head over heels in love you fall suddenly and deeply in love with someone.

It was obvious that Alan had fallen head over heels in love with Veronica.

When I was 18 I fell head over heels for my next-door neighbor, Alex.

NOTE You can also say that someone is head over heels or is head over heels in love.

It's plain from the tone in Colin's voice that he's head over heels.

You have to remember that I was head over heels in love with Bill.

NOTE Until the late 18th century this expression was 'heels over head', which refers to someone doing a somersault (=turning over in the air).

have a soft spot for someone/something

If you have a soft spot for someone or something, you like them.

The actress has admitted having a soft spot for our future King.

I've always had a soft spot for roses – my Dad used to grow them when I was a child.

head and shoulders above someone/something

If one person or thing is head and shoulders above others of their kind, they are much better than them.

In the world of newspaper publishing there is one success story that stands head and shoulders above the rest.

Richards, according to Imran Khan, was head and shoulders above any other player.

no great shakes

If someone or something is no great shakes they are not skilful or of good quality. [INFORMAL]

She can write screenplays well enough but she's no great shakes as a director.

NOTE This expression probably refers to shaking dice and getting a poor result, although there are other possible explanations.

nothing to write home about or not much to write home about

If something is nothing to write home about or not much to write home about it is not very interesting, exciting or special. [INFORMAL]

The house was nothing to write home about – a rather scruffy Victorian semi-detached like many they'd seen.

The nightlife is not much to write home about.

of your dreams

If someone or something is the person or thing of your dreams, they are the best you can imagine.

Maybe, just maybe, the man of your dreams will walk through that door and into your life tonight.

an old flame

An old flame is someone who you had a romantic relationship with in the past.

NOTE   An old meaning of 'flame' was the person that someone was in love with.

Last week Alec was seen dining with his old flame Janine Turner in New York.

not a patch on someone/something

If one person or thing is not a patch on another, the first is not nearly as good as the second. [INFORMAL]

NOTE   This is probably a shortened version of 'not fit to be a patch on', suggesting a small piece of cloth that is not of good enough quality to be used to mend a hole in a good piece of clothing.

He was handsome, she thought, but not a patch on Alex.

a saving grace

A saving grace is a good quality or feature in someone or something that prevents them from being completely bad or worthless.

It's an excellent performance and one of the film's few saving graces.

there are plenty more fish in the sea or there are other fish in the sea

If you tell someone that there are plenty more fish in the sea or there are other fish in the sea you mean that there are many other people they could have a relationship with.

Tell him there are plenty more fish in the sea and he's sure to find the perfect woman.

NOTE   This expression can vary.

Remember that there are many more fish in the sea.

think the world of someone

If you think the world of someone you like and admire them very much or are very fond of them.

He thinks the world of his little grandson.

you have to be cruel to be kind

When people say you have to be cruel to be kind they mean that sometimes if you are unkind to someone it will be the best thing for them.

'I have to be cruel to be kind' said Lindsay. 'If I don't control his food he will gain too much weight.'

Exercise 1

Complete the sentences with the words in the box.

| spot | flame | home | grace | head | torch | patch | dreams |

1 We've known each other for years and I've always had a soft _____ for Gerri.
2 We didn't think her new boyfriend was a _____ on the one she had before.
3 I found a photo of my dad with an old _____ from his college days.
4 She carried a _____ for the boy next door all through their teenage years.
5 Yes, I suppose he's good-looking, but not really much to write _____ about.
6 You can see they're _____ over heels in love with each other.
7 It was in Tunisia that they saw the house of their _____.
8 I don't like her but the fact that she loves him so much is her saving _____.

Exercise 2

Answer the questions.

1 If you carry a torch for someone, are you in love with them or are they in love with you?
2 If something is a common-or-garden, is it ordinary or special?
3 If something is no great shakes, does it impress you?
4 If you are head and shoulders above someone else, are they better, or not as good as you at something?
5 If someone has a soft spot for you, do they like or dislike you?
6 If someone is not a patch on you, are they better or worse than you?

Exercise 3

Choose the best idiom to match the sentences.

1 We don't allow her to go out with her friends on school nights during exam time.

   a she's nothing to write home about   b you have to be cruel to be kind

   c there are plenty more fish in the sea

2 The first time they met he knew she was the one for him.

   a she's nothing to write home about   b he fell head over heels in love
   c she was an old flame

3 His mother won't let anyone criticize him.

   a she carries a torch for him   b she's head over heels   c she thinks the world of him

4 I expect he'll find another girlfriend pretty soon.

   a there are plenty more fish in the sea   b he's nothing to write home about
   c you have to be cruel to be kind

5 He's the best player this team has ever had.
   a there are other fish in the sea   b he's not a patch on the others
   c he's head and shoulders above the others

6 He's very creative in the kitchen but _____ on the management side of the business.

   a head over heels   b no great shakes   c an old flame

Exercise 4

Re-order the phrases to make sentences. Add punctuation where necessary.

1 and I / my piano teacher / thought the world of her / was a lovely woman
2 he's a genius / a common-or-garden teaching job / he has / but I think
3 with a girl / a friend of mine / he met on holiday / fell head over heels in love
4 it's nothing to write home about / but frankly, / we have a new car that / cost a lot of money
5 a memory of / do you have / an old flame / that is precious to you
6 it's a good film but / the film / that inspired it / it's not a patch on

Exercise 5

Replace the <u>underlined</u> words and phrases with the idioms in the box.

old flame | saving grace | of their dreams | had a soft spot for | not a patch on
nothing to write home about | thinks the world of | head and shoulders above

1 They spent their evenings planning the holiday <u>they would most like to take</u>.
2 The clothes are awful but they have one <u>good feature</u>: they will not wear out.
3 My results are okay, but <u>not exceptional</u>.
4 I've always <u>cared a lot about</u> her.
5 Apparently James is an <u>ex boyfriend</u> of Amanda's.
6 He <u>adores</u> his grandmother.
7 His new girlfriend is <u>not nearly as wonderful as</u> his last girlfriend.
8 There was one applicant who was <u>far better than all</u> the rest.

Exercise 6

Complete the table. Put the idioms in the correct groups.

fall head over heels (in love) | common-or-garden | have a soft spot for someone | an old flame
no great shakes | head and shoulders above someone/something | carry a torch for someone
think the world of someone | nothing to write home about

romantic love	1 _____
	2 _____
	3 _____
liking or admiring someone or something	1 _____
	2 _____
	3 _____
not being very special	1 _____
	2 _____
	3 _____

Your turn!

Think about the people and things in your life that you love and like. Use the idioms in this unit to talk about them. For example:

I think the world of my English teacher.

This house is not a patch on the one we used to live in.

Has anyone seen my glasses?

Oh, how sweet!

He was sometimes absent-minded but she still **had a soft spot for him.**

24

Happiness and sadness

break someone's heart

1 If you break someone's heart you make them very unhappy by ending a relationship with them or making it clear that you do not love them.

She left him later that year and broke his heart.

> NOTE   You can also say that someone has a broken heart when they feel very sad because a relationship has ended.

If you're a poet, you get some good poetry out of a broken heart.

> NOTE   You can also say that someone is heartbroken or is broken-hearted.

Mary was broken-hearted when he left her.

2 If a fact or a situation breaks your heart it makes you very sad.

It broke my heart to see this woman suffer the way she did.

> NOTE   You can also say that someone is heartbroken or is broken-hearted if they are very upset about something.

down in the dumps or in the dumps

If you are down in the dumps or in the dumps you feel depressed.

Try to support each other when one of you is feeling down in the dumps.

I was in the dumps when I met Jayne. I was clearly not living the kind of life I should live.

full of beans

If you are full of beans you are very happy and energetic.

> NOTE   This originally referred to a horse that was well-fed and therefore full of energy.

Jem was among them, full of beans after his long sleep.

get a kick out of something

If you get a kick out of something you enjoy it very much. [INFORMAL]

These doctors take on huge workloads and get a kick out of being busy, helping people, curing patients and saving lives.

get on top of you

If something gets on top of you it makes you feel sad or upset, and you are not able to deal with it.

I was so fed up. Everything was just getting on top of me.

have a whale of a time

If you have a whale of a time, you enjoy yourself a lot. [INFORMAL]

Kids of all ages will have a whale of a time at the amusement park.

a long face

If someone has a long face they look very serious or unhappy.

He came to me with a very long face and admitted there had been an error.

look on the bright side

If you look on the bright side you try to be cheerful about a bad situation by concentrating on the few good things in it or by thinking about how it could have been even worse.

I tried to look on the bright side, to be grateful that I was at least healthy.

NOTE   You can also just talk about a bright side of a bad situation.

There is a bright side to this depressing situation, at least for one group of people: American tourists. They're getting more for their dollar right now.

make someone's day

If someone or something makes your day they make you feel very happy.

There was such a sincere expression of friendliness on both their faces that it was a joy to see. It really made my day.

not a happy bunny

If you say that someone is not a happy bunny you mean that they are annoyed or unhappy about something. [BRITISH, INFORMAL]

NOTE   'Bunny' is a childish word for a rabbit and the expression is meant to sound like part of a children's story. It is used humorously.

I'm receiving around 100 junk emails a day. I'm not a happy bunny.

on top of the world

If you feel on top of the world you feel extremely happy.

The combination of cold, crisp snow and warm sunshine makes you feel on top of the world.

over the moon

If you are over the moon about something that has happened you are very happy about it. [mainly BRITISH, INFORMAL]

'Caroline must be pleased about her new job?' 'Yes, she's over the moon.'

a shoulder to cry on

A shoulder to cry on is someone who is sympathetic to you when you are upset and listens when you talk about your problems.

For a lot of new mums the health visitor is the perfect shoulder to cry on when it all gets too much.

NOTE   You can also say that one person cries on another's shoulder.

He had let her cry on his shoulder when her mother died, taking her calls in the middle of the night.

Exercise 1

Choose the best answer to complete the sentences.

1 Look on the _____ side. You still have a job.

   a good   b bright   c top

2 I'm over the _____ about Rosie's news.

   a moon   b world   c side

3 Why have you got such a _____ face?

   a long   b bad   c low

4 He always gets a _____ out of being recognized in the street.

   a hit   b kick   c whale

5 Don't let that dreary job get on _____ of you.

   a down   b side   c top

6 He's been looking very down in the _____ lately.

   a face   b world   c dumps

7 She's become her old self again – laughing and full of _____.

   a kicks   b beans   c dumps

8 She was on top of the _____, showing everyone her engagement ring.

   a world   b moon   c time

Exercise 2

Match sentence halves 1–6 with A–F to make complete sentences.

1 You made my day when

2 He felt full of beans after

3 She was on top of the world because

4 Everyone needs a shoulder to cry on when

5 She broke her mother's heart when

6 The bright side is that you can

A she'd been invited for an interview.

B you told me how beautiful I was.

C they've had depressing news.

D he'd had a steam bath and massage.

E visit them for your holidays.

F she decided to give up dancing.

Exercise 3

Complete the advertisements with the words in the box.

| HAVE | OVER | DOWN | MAKE | FULL | TOP |

1 _____ SOMEONE'S DAY – GIVE THEM A BOOK TOKEN!

2 DON'T LET ILLNESS GET ON _____ OF YOU – STAY FIT AND HEALTHY

3 GIVE YOUR WIFE FLOWERS ON VALENTINE'S DAY – SHE'LL BE _____ THE MOON

4 START THE DAY WITH WHEATIES CEREAL – BE _____ OF BEANS ALL DAY!

5 SPRING TIME ALLERGIES? NO NEED TO BE _____ IN THE DUMPS WITH OUR NEW TREATMENT

6 TRY OUR NEW SWIMMING POOL AND _____ A WHALE OF A TIME!

Exercise 4

Complete the sentences. Choose the correct answers.

1 Something must be wrong. Sally looks *over the moon* / *down in the dumps* / *full of beans*.

2 The meeting didn't go well – it was awful. I'm *not a happy bunny* / *getting a kick out of it* / *full of beans*.

3 I love doing Sudoku puzzles! *They really get on top of me* / *I really get a kick out of them* / *They break my heart*.

4 I'm sorry about your news. I'm here, if you need *a shoulder to cry on* / *a long face* / *to get a kick out of something*.

5 I know you've got a lot of work but you'll manage. Just don't let it *make your day* / *look on the bright side* / *get on top of you*.

6 Thanks for telling me that great news. It really *broke my heart* / *made my day* / *got on top of me*.

Exercise 5

Match idioms A–F with situations 1–3.

1 enjoying something   □ □
2 being unhappy   □ □
3 being very happy   □ □

A She was over the moon when she heard the news.
B Carl's walking around with a very long face today.
C I really get a kick out of being on stage.
D Tina's been very down in the dumps lately.
E They're having a whale of a time.
F He's on top of the world at the moment.

Exercise 6

Correct the idioms in these sentences.

1 If you need an arm to cry on, you know where I am.
2 When she came back from that holiday she was on the top of the world.
3 Business hasn't been good and things have been getting on top of my head lately.
4 When you have a customer who turns round and thanks you, it builds your day.
5 Khaled has been up in the dumps since failing his exam.
6 It was easy to see that Kari was not a funny bunny.
7 He left rather hurriedly but when he came back he was made of beans.
8 She was over the side when she heard their news.

Exercise 7

Complete the sentences with idioms from this unit, changing the pronouns and verb forms if necessary.

1 Give me a ring any time if you feel you need _____.
2 I took one look at his _____ and knew something was wrong.
3 She _____ by offering to make the dinner.
4 Things could be so much worse; you have to _____.
5 He's one of those nasty individuals who _____ bad things happening to other people.
6 My father didn't want me to leave home and it _____ when I did go, at seventeen.
7 We all _____ at Fahida's birthday party.
8 You look a bit _____. What's wrong?

Your turn!

Think about what makes you happy or sad. Use the idioms in this unit to describe any of your experiences. For example:

I sometimes feel a bit down in the dumps when I don't get enough exercise.

I get a big kick out of doing well in English tests.

Because her dog was **full of beans**, taking him for a walk was easy!

101

Health, illness, and death

alive and kicking

If someone or something is alive and kicking they are still active or still exist.

Romance is still alive and kicking for a couple who will be celebrating their 50th wedding anniversary this week.

The twins want to let everyone know who has written to them that they are alive and kicking.

at death's door

If someone is at death's door they are seriously ill and likely to die.

He has won five golf competitions in three months, a year after being at death's door.

NOTE You can also say that someone is near death's door.

The singer said he was 'active and feeling very well' as he responded to reports that he was near death's door.

NOTE You can say that someone comes back from death's door or is brought back from death's door when they have recovered from a very serious illness.

The patient has been brought back from death's door by the new treatment, say his doctors.

a clean bill of health

If someone is given or gets a clean bill of health they are told that they are completely fit and healthy.

NOTE A bill of health was a certificate which was given to a ship's captain to present at the next port the ship arrived at. It stated whether or not there was an infectious disease aboard the ship or in the port it was departing from.

He had a full medical examination late last year and was given a clean bill of health.

be dropping like flies

If people are dropping like flies, large numbers of them are falling ill or dying within a short period of time.

Actors his age – many of them friends – were dropping like flies.

end it all

If someone ends it all they kill themselves.

Boring, grey stage lighting can be ideal if your heroine is just about to end it all.

NOTE This expression is usually used in a humorous way.

be fighting for your life

If someone is fighting for their life they are seriously ill or injured and are in danger of dying.

A boy aged 15 was fighting for his life last night but two younger children were said to be out of danger.

NOTE You can also talk about a fight for life.

Mary won a desperate fight for life and went on to make a full recovery.

kick the bucket

If someone kicks the bucket they die. [INFORMAL]

> NOTE   The origins of this expression are uncertain. One suggestion is that the 'bucket' was a wooden frame which was used when killing livestock. The animals were hung from the bucket by their back legs. After they had been killed their legs often continued to twitch and kick against the bucket. Ironically, this expression is now used in a humorous way.

Our neighbor is about to kick the bucket – *he has some sort of kidney infection.*

knock someone for six

[1] If something knocks you for six it shocks or upsets you so much that you have difficulty recovering. [BRITISH, INFORMAL]

The emotional shock of losing a parent can knock you for six.

[2] If an illness knocks you for six it causes you to be very ill and weak for a long time.

I picked up a virus that knocked me for six. *I lost a stone in weight in two weeks.*

> NOTE   In cricket, six runs are scored when a batsman hits the ball so that it lands outside the playing area without bouncing. When this happens you can say the bowler has been hit for six.

a shadow of your former self

If someone is a shadow of their former self they are very much thinner than they used to be.

I couldn't believe how much weight she'd lost – she's a shadow of her former self.

skin and bone or skin and bones

If you describe someone as skin and bone or skin and bones you mean that they are very thin, usually because they are ill.

A man like me can't live on beans – I'll soon be skin and bone.

By the end of her life she was nothing but skin and bones.

under the weather

If you are under the weather you are feeling ill.

I'd been feeling a bit under the weather *for a couple of weeks.*

a wake-up call

A wake-up call is something which shocks people, making them understand how serious a problem is and causing them to take action in order to solve that problem.

> NOTE   If you have a wake-up call, you arrange for someone to telephone you at a certain time in the morning so that you are sure to wake up at that time.

The report should be a wake-up call *for governments around the world to take action to improve healthcare resources for young people.*

the worse for wear

If someone is the worse for wear they are tired or injured.

In the fourth round both fighters suffered cuts over the eyes, and the champion was beginning to look the worse for wear.

Exercise 1

Complete the sentences with the words in the box.

death | health | life | wear | alive | end | kick | knock

1 He lay at _____'s door for months but made a miraculous recovery.
2 After a year of illness I finally have a clean bill of _____.
3 My father is still _____ and kicking at 85.
4 She told me that she wasn't ready to _____ the bucket yet.
5 The man involved in the accident is fighting for his _____ in the local hospital.
6 A minor infection can _____ you for six if you don't look after yourself.
7 It's been a heavy week and now I'm feeling a bit the worse for _____.
8 She went through some bad times but never felt she wanted to _____ it all.

Exercise 2

Re-order the phrases to make sentences. Add punctuation where necessary.

1 the members of / were dropping like flies / the golf club / with food poisoning
2 was delighted / the manager / a clean bill of health / to receive / for his team
3 her music career / in spite of / is alive and kicking / her problems
4 terribly / was a wake-up call / the heart attack / that scared him
5 from stress and / was generally / she was suffering / under the weather
6 to see / had become / that Bill / I was shocked / a shadow of his former self

Exercise 3

Choose the best answer to complete the sentences.

1 They all thought he would die but he's still _____.

  a alive and kicking   b kicking the bucket   c knocking himself for six

2 The woman was 71, living on a small pension and she was nothing but _____.

  a under the weather   b skin and bones   c alive and kicking

3 For one brief moment he considered _____, but he knew everything would eventually get better.

  a ending it all   b kicking the bucket   c living and kicking

4 I suffered from a virus that _____.

  a kicked my bucket   b fought for my life   c knocked me for six

5 The illness has reduced him to _____.

  a a shadow of his former self   b a clean bill of health   c a wake-up call

6 You might be _____ but you should still turn up if you can.

  a fighting for your life   b under the weather   c alive and kicking

Exercise 4

Replace the <u>underlined</u> words with words and phrases in the box with the same meaning.

it knocked him for a six | under the weather | wake-up call | fighting for his life
skin and bone | given a clean bill of health

1 After the accident, he was in hospital, <u>in a critical condition</u>.
2 I've been <u>declared completely well</u> by my doctor.
3 Are you feeling alright? You look a bit <u>unwell</u>.
4 Has she been ill? She's <u>so thin</u>!
5 Having that heart attack was a <u>warning signal</u> – he now takes his health much more seriously.
6 The news really upset him – <u>he hasn't fully recovered from the shock yet</u>.

Exercise 5

Correct the idioms in these sentences.

1 The old folk around here have been fighting like flies recently.
2 He really changed after his wife's death. He's a shade of his former self.
3 I'll have to take the day off work – I'm a bit worse for health today.
4 Apparently she was really ill – at death's knock, in fact – but she's fine now.
5 You'll be pleased to know that all the new-born puppies are alive and living!
6 Two people were killed in the accident, and one is still fighting for his health.

Exercise 6

Arrange the idioms in pairs to complete the table.

a shadow of your former self | alive and kicking | under the weather | skin and bone/s
be fighting for your life | end it all | the worse for wear | a clean bill of heath
at death's door | kick the bucket

being well	1 _____
	2 _____
being unwell	1 _____
	2 _____
being thin	1 _____
	2 _____
almost dying	1 _____
	2 _____
dying	1 _____
	2 _____

Your turn!

Have health issues affected you recently? Use the idioms in this unit to describe any of your experiences. For example:

I felt like I was at death's door when I had the flu last month.

I often feel the worse for wear in the morning if I don't go to bed early enough.

He was finding it hard to accept the flower was **at death's door.**

Appendix 1   Understanding idioms

Like most language learners you may often find idioms difficult to understand. Even though you may understand all of the words in an idiom, when they are put together and used figuratively, it can be difficult to work out the meaning.

Imagery

One of the main reasons learners find idioms difficult to understand is that unlike native speakers, they are not familiar with the image that the idiom is based on. In *Work on your Idioms*, information on the image the idiom is based on is included in the Note sections. These will help you to understand where the idiom comes from as well as help you to remember it.

---

from the horse's mouth

If you get a piece of information from the horse's mouth, you get it directly from someone who is involved in it and knows the most about it.

NOTE   This expression may refer to the fact that you can tell a horse's age by looking at its teeth.

When he tells them, straight from the horse's mouth, what a good assistant you are, they'll increase your wages.

There are other ways of explaining idioms and if you are aware of these, they will help you understand idioms you come across more easily.

Shared physical experience

Some idioms are based on a shared physical experience. For example, butterflies in your stomach (Unit 13).

---

butterflies in your stomach

If you have butterflies in your stomach, you feel very nervous about something that you have to do.

Now I've qualified as a competitor, I'm starting to feel the butterflies in my stomach already.

This idiom uses the image of butterflies fluttering in your stomach to describe how you feel when you are nervous about something. We can all relate to this because as humans we have a strange feeling in our stomachs when we are anxious about something.

As a language learner, you may find these kinds of idioms easier to remember because the shared physical experience might be the same in your culture and you may even have a similar idiom in your mother tongue. However be aware that you cannot always assume that the idiom in your mother tongue has the same meaning in English and that you can translate word for word. Here are some other idioms from this book that are based on a shared physical experience.

be shaking like a leaf (Unit 13)
jump out of your skin (Unit 13)

Specific areas of experience

Another way to understand idioms is to identify the specific area of experience that the idiom is based on. For example, some idioms are based on sport, war, cooking or films. Cut to the chase (Unit 4) is based on the area of films.

> ### cut to the chase
>
> If you cut to the chase, you start talking about or dealing with what is really important, instead of less important things.
>
> NOTE   In films, when one scene ends and another begins the action is said to 'cut' from one scene to the next. If a film 'cuts to the chase', it moves on to a car chase scene, which is usually fast-moving and exciting.
>
> *I'll cut to the chase – we just don't have enough money for the project.*

If you know which specific area of experience the idiom is based on, it is easier to remember the meaning. Grouping idioms in your notebook under their specific area of experience may help you to remember them more easily. Also, if you recognize the origin of a new idiom, you might be able to work out its meaning on your own. Developing these skills is useful. Here are some other idioms from this book that are based on experience in sport.

a level playing field (Unit 10)
move the goalposts (Unit 10)
par for the course (Unit 17)

Historical/Cultural context

It is also useful to think about the historical/cultural context of idioms. For example, English has lots of idioms that are based on sailing because historically England was a seafaring nation. Knowing this will help you recognize and understand idioms with their origins in sailing. Here are some examples from this book.

plain sailing (Unit 15)
the coast is clear (Unit 19)

Similarly, for historical/cultural reasons, there are lots of idioms in the English language that are based on card games, horse racing and hunting. Here are some examples from this book.

above board (Unit 10)
leave someone in the lurch (Unit 5)

Simile

Many idioms in English are based on similes. A simile is an expression that describes a person or thing as being similar to someone or something else. This comparison often makes these idioms easier to remember. Here are some examples from this book.

a mind like a sieve (Unit 2)
get on like a house on fire (Unit 5)
treat someone like dirt (Unit 5)

Sound patterns

Up to 20 per cent of English idioms use alliteration (where the initial letters or sounds of all, or most of words are the same) or use words that rhyme. Because of the sound patterns of these idioms they can be easier to remember. Here are some examples from this book.

make a mountain out of a molehill (Unit 4)
a labour of love (Unit 7)
break your back (Unit 9)
below the belt (Unit 10)
fair and square (Unit 10)

Appendix 2 Study tips

Here are some practical study tips for remembering idioms.

Break the idiom down into parts

This should help you to learn and remember the form of the idiom.

Look, Say, Cover, Write, Check

Another way to learn idioms is to go through these five stages:

- Look at the idiom carefully.
- Say the idiom aloud to yourself, listening to how it sounds.
- Cover the idiom and try to remember what it looks like.
- Write the idiom.
- Check what you have written to see if you got it right.

Pictures

Many idioms are based on images, and having a picture in your memory can help you to remember the idiom. You could draw pictures in your notebook to help you remember the image that the idiom creates. The illustrations that appear in this book will help you, too.

Stories

When you watch a film or TV programme in English, listen for idioms and try to remember them in that context. For example, if a character in a film says 'You're pulling my leg!', try to remember the situation with that idiom. What was the joke? Was it really a joke? Did the character ever believe what they'd been told?

The story:

- helps you to understand how the idiom is used
- shows you the kind of people who use the idiom: their relationships how they feel when they use it
- shows you that the situation is a good time to use that idiom, so that you will be able to use it when you are in a similar situation
- allows you to keep a mental picture that will help you remember the expression.

Look and listen

Look and listen for the idioms that you have seen or heard before. When you read or hear one, spend a moment checking that you understand how it is being used in this new context.

Try to carry a notebook with you (a good idea for learning all new vocabulary) and make a note of the idiom and the context that you heard or read it in. If you are reading a text and it's appropriate, you could underline any idioms that appear in the text and look these up in a dictionary later.

Organizing your notebook

The idioms presented in this book have been grouped in topics to make them easier to remember and to help you use and understand them in everyday situations. As mentioned above, you can also organize your notebook according to the origin of the meaning of the idiom. So you could group idioms that you come across under the following headings:

* Shared physical experience
* Specific areas of experience
* Historical/Cultural context
* Simile
* Sound patterns

Practise and revision

Find opportunities to practise whenever you can, and make an effort to use the idioms you've been studying.

You have to be patient while learning idioms. You can't use them anywhere and in any sentence. If you use them incorrectly, idioms can sound funny, so trying them and asking questions can be helpful. Develop a habit of making sentences including idioms and trying them out. That will help you to remember them properly.

Research tells us that actively using and revising new vocabulary helps you to store the information in your long-term memory. Students who learn best:

* find opportunities to try out new words in real-life communication – this is likely to be more effective than 'safer' contexts such as the classroom or private study
* ask questions to check what they know about words
* test themselves
* revise regularly – 'little and often' is better than occasional, large-scale revision.

Appendix 3 American English alternatives

The majority of the idioms in this book are common to both British and American varieties of English. Sometimes you may see a label [BRITISH]. This means that this idiom is mainly used in British English. In this section you can find some of the idioms from the units that have American English alternatives. An example sentence for the American English alternative is also given.

common-or-garden (Unit 23)

[AMERICAN] **garden variety**

NOTE   Both these idioms are used like adjectives. They originally referred to plants and have developed differently in each variety of English.

The experiment itself is garden-variety science that normally would attract little public attention.

be flogging a dead horse (Unit 16)

[AMERICAN] **be beating a dead horse**

NOTE   'Flogging' is always used in British English, and 'beating' in American English.

You're beating a dead horse here. These guys are definitely already defeated.

not get a word in edgeways (Unit 13)

[AMERICAN] **not get a word in edgewise**

NOTE   Where people say 'edgeways' in British English, 'edgewise' is the form that is used in American English.

Jamie dominated the conversation and Zhou could hardly get a word in edgewise.

go back a long way (Unit 5)

[AMERICAN] **go way back**

NOTE   This is a set phrase in both versions. Both are used in British English.

This here is Dan Parker. We go way back.

a grey area (Unit 1)

[AMERICAN] **a gray area**

NOTE   'Grey' is usually spelled 'gray' in American English.

He complained about the way Hollywood reduced the complex gray areas of life to black and white.

have an axe to grind (Unit 7)

[AMERICAN] **have an ax to grind**

NOTE   'Axe' is spelled 'ax' in American English.

If you have an ax to grind or feel strongly about something, the job of trying to get something done may become a lot easier if you go online.

the icing on the cake (Unit 4)

[AMERICAN] **the frosting on the cake**

NOTE   'Frosting' is the American English word for icing.

If you become friends after you have enjoyed a good professional relationship, that is the frosting on the cake.

in the pipeline (Unit 16)

[AMERICAN] in the works

> NOTE   The idiom means exactly the same but 'the works' in the American English version refers to the working parts of a machine, so that the image is of something being manufactured or produced. The use of 'pipeline' in the British English version focuses more on the movement of something that is due to arrive at some point in the future. Obviously, both versions are about development and processes.

They confirmed a deal that's been in the works *for several weeks.*

in two minds (Unit 4)

[AMERICAN] of two minds

> *Kennedy was* of two minds *about the plan, but in the end he authorized it.*

lead someone up the garden path (Unit 11)

[AMERICAN] lead someone down the garden path

> *They* led me down the garden path *and made me believe there would be a job for me.*

on the cards (Unit 17)

[AMERICAN] in the cards

> *There's no need to look so surprised. It's been* in the cards, *as they say, for a long time.*

plain sailing (Unit 15)

[AMERICAN] smooth sailing, clear sailing, easy sailing

> NOTE   In British English, only 'plain sailing' is used, whereas in American English there are several choices.

> *All of a sudden, my life started to improve, which is not to say that it was all* smooth sailing *from then on.*

> *Their twenty-four year relationship hasn't always been* clear sailing.

put your foot in it (Unit 18)

[AMERICAN] put your foot in your mouth

> NOTE   Both versions refer to being clumsy. Perhaps the British English version is easier to relate to a situation, whereas the American English idea focuses more on actually saying something inappropriate or embarrassing.

This man should have a press adviser to stop him from continuously putting his foot in his mouth.

sweep something under the carpet (Unit 11)

[AMERICAN] sweep something under the rug

> NOTE   A rug is smaller than a carpet, but the idea is obviously the same.

You can't just sweep this problem under the rug.

wear the trousers (Unit 21)

[AMERICAN ENGLISH] wear the pants

> NOTE   In American English, 'pants' means 'trousers'. In British English, 'pants' means 'underpants', so although these versions seem different, they mean exactly the same both idiomatically and literally.

My father said he wanted to discuss the investment with my mother, to which the salesman demanded, 'Who wears the pants *in your family?'*

Answer key

1 Knowledge and understanding

Exercise 1

1 hang
2 clue
3 area
4 stick
5 ear
6 picture

Exercise 2

1 D
2 B
3 A
4 F
5 E
6 C

Exercise 3

1 get the picture
2 up to speed
3 get my head round it
4 get the hang of it
5 jump to conclusions
6 have a clue

Exercise 4

1 get the picture
2 get the wrong end of the stick
3 haven't got a clue
4 read between the lines
5 get the hang of it
6 go in one ear and out the other

Exercise 5

1 Stefan's
2 Xavier
3 Khalid
4 Nik
5 Cheng
6 Veejay

Exercise 6

understanding correctly	get your head around something
	up to speed
	take something on board
	read between the lines
	get the hang of something
	get the picture
	put two and two together
not understanding	not have a clue
	get the wrong end of the stick
	a grey area
	jump to conclusions
	go in one ear and out the other

2 Memory and mind

Exercise 1

1 brain *OR* mind
2 head
3 mind
4 thought
5 head
6 brain *OR* brains

Exercise 2

1 F
2 T
3 F
4 F
5 T
6 F

Exercise 3

1 b
2 c
3 c
4 b
5 a
6 b

Exercise 4

1 lost the plot
2 bear in mind
3 off your head *OR* out of your mind
4 Off the top of his head
5 food for thought
6 on the tip of my tongue
7 gut reaction
8 crossed my mind

Exercise 5

1 G
2 F
3 B
4 C
5 D
6 E
7 H
8 A

Exercise 6

Possible answers

remembering and forgetting	a mind/brain like a sieve ring a bell bear/keep something mind off the top of your head on the tip of your tongue
thinking	food for thought rack your brain(s) cross your mind miles away
not thinking logically	a gut reaction lose the plot off/out of your head out of your mind

Exercise 6

Possible answers

communicating badly	go off at/on a tangent get your wires crossed at cross purposes
maintaining communication	keep someone in the picture keep someone posted in the loop touch base
revealing a secret	let the cat out of the bag spill the beans
trusting information	hear something on the grapevine from the horse´s mouth in black and white

3 Communicating

Exercise 1

1	C	5	D
2	H	6	B
3	G	7	A
4	F	8	E

Exercise 2

1	in	5	from
2	at / on	6	at
3	on	7	out
4	in	8	out

Exercise 3

1 It must be true because it's here in black and white.

2 Keep me in the loop as you develop the idea.

3 We meet every week to have lunch and touch base.

4 I thought that the discussion was moving off on a tangent.

5 She asked him to keep her posted on how she was doing.

6 The newspaper reporter paid the office cleaner to spill the beans.

7 They managed to find common ground on the issue of rates of pay.

8 The family agreed that going away to university would bring him out of his shell.

Exercise 4

1	C	4	E
2	A	5	F
3	B	6	D

Exercise 5

1	D	4	E
2	F	5	A
3	B	6	C

4 Priorities and decisions

Exercise 1

1	by	4	in
2	of	5	to
3	on	6	to

Exercise 2

1	E	4	C
2	D	5	A
3	F	6	B

Exercise 3

1	a	4	c
2	c	5	c
3	b	6	b

Exercise 4

1 up in the air

2 tip of the iceberg

3 stick to your guns

4 cross that bridge

5 play it by ear

6 is the bottom line

7 take a back seat

8 the icing on the cake

Exercise 5

1 the icing on the cake

2 up in the air

3 play it by ear

4 cut to the chase

5 the tip of the iceberg

6 sit on the fence

7 make a mountain out of a molehill

8 take a back seat

Exercise 6

Possible answers

emphasizing something important	the bottom line
	cut to the chase
showing that something is less important	make a mountain out of a molehill
	split hairs
	on the back burner
	the icing on the cake
a decision not yet made	play it by ear
	sit on the fence
	up in the air
	in two minds

5 Relationships

Exercise 1

1 B, E, F

2 D

Exercise 2

1 B		5 C	
2 F		6 H	
3 A		7 D	
4 E		8 G	

Exercise 3

1 c

2 b

3 c

4 a

5 a

6 b

Exercise 4

1 gave me the cold <u>shoulder</u>

2 we're getting on like a house on <u>fire</u>

3 go back <u>a long way</u>

4 hit it <u>off</u>

5 gets on my <u>nerves</u>

6 on the same <u>wavelength</u>

Exercise 5

1 sparks fly

2 leave you in the lurch

3 got off on the wrong foot

4 break the ice

5 hit it off

6 treats him like dirt

7 save face

8 her own flesh and blood

Exercise 6

successful relationships	go back a long way
	get on like a house on fire
	hit it off
	on the same wavelength
bad relationships	get off on the wrong foot
	sparks fly
	give someone the cold shoulder
	get on someone's nerves
	leave someone in the lurch
	on the rocks
	treat someone like dirt

6 Help and encouragement

Exercise 1

1 on

2 together

3 in

4 over

5 under

6 up

Exercise 2

1 b		3 b		5 a	
2 a		4 c		6 a	

Exercise 3

1 help them

2 cheerful

3 pleased

4 trying to help them

5 they are being helpful to you

6 give help

Exercise 4

1 The party bends over backwards to attract women candidates.

2 Girls and boys learn that there must be give and take in all relationships.

3 The whole family has to lend a hand with the harvest.

4 They must put their heads together in order to reach a sensible decision.

5 You know I'll always be there for you.

6 What should we do if our elected representatives choose to look the other way?

Exercise 5

1 C		5 B	
2 H		6 A	
3 E		7 D	
4 F		8 G	

Exercise 6

1 Maria

2 Smith and Burnet

3 Sven

4 Ewen

5 Rakesh

6 Manuelle

7 Sasha

8 Lisa

7 Involvement and interest

Exercise 1

1 c   4 a

2 b   5 c

3 b   6 a

Exercise 2

1 D   4 E

2 C   5 F

3 B   6 A

Exercise 3

1 T   4 T

2 F   5 T

3 F   6 F

Exercise 4

1 b   4 b

2 a   5 a

3 a   6 b

Exercise 5

1 up to my ears

2 mean business

3 jump on the band wagon

4 have an axe to grind

5 steer clear of

6 not really my cup of tea

Exercise 6

1 keep a low profile

2 mean business

3 poke their noses into

4 jump on the bandwagon

5 steer clear of

6 try my hand

7 whetted my appetite

8 nosy parker

Exercise 7

1 labour of love

2 meant business

3 keep a low profile

4 have an axe to grind

5 poke/stick your nose into

6 steered clear of

7 up to their ears

8 Try your hand

8 Starting and stopping

Exercise 1

1 ball

2 leaf

3 ground

4 head

5 halt

6 bud

7 day

8 business

Exercise 2

1 D   4 B

2 C   5 F

3 E   6 A

Exercise 3

1 ground to a halt

2 call it a day

3 turned over a new leaf

4 knocked it on the head

5 hit the ground running

6 start from scratch

Exercise 4

1 C   4 E

2 B   5 F

3 A   6 D

Exercise 5

1 call it a day

2 you're in business

3 from scratch

4 enough is enough

5 cut my losses

6 call it quits

7 up and running

8 nip it in the bud

Exercise 6

1 E   4 A

2 B   5 D

3 F   6 C

Exercise 7

Possible answers

starting	set/start the ball rolling
	hit the ground running
	in business
	from scratch
	up and running
stopping	nip something in the bud
	call it a day
	grind to a halt
	knock something on the head
	call it quits
	enough is enough
	cut your losses
both	turn over a new leaf

9 Effort

Exercise 1

1 corners

2 feet

3 socks

4 candle

5 halves

6 finger

7 socks

8 fingers

Exercise 2

1 a	3 c	5 b
2 c	4 b	6 a

Exercise 3

1 After last week's triumph, the team are ready to go all out for another win. *OR*
   The team are ready to go all out for another win after last week's triumph.

2 There are millions of people who have to work their fingers to the bone just to stay alive.

3 We will have to play our socks off if we want to beat them. *OR*
   If we want to beat them we will have to play our socks off.

4 It's better not to try to do things cheaply by cutting corners.

5 He had a bit of trouble but it looks like he'll land on his feet.

6 The newspapers just love to make a meal of a story like this.

Exercise 4

1 C	4 B
2 E	5 A
3 F	6 D

Exercise 5

1 George

2 Jean

3 Ellana

4 Helen

5 Kaz

6 Anton

7 Kiri

8 Anna

Exercise 6

1 breaking my back

2 landed on her feet

3 making a meal

4 go the extra mile

5 lift a finger

6 working my socks off

7 pulls their weight

8 never did anything by halves

10 Honesty and fairness

Exercise 1

1 nose

2 means

3 level

4 table

5 board

6 clean

7 belt

8 bush

Exercise 2

1 T	5 T
2 F	6 F
3 F	7 F
4 F	8 T

Exercise 3

1 D	5 E
2 C	6 G
3 H	7 F
4 A	8 B

Exercise 4

1 fair and square

2 beating around the bush

3 below the belt

4 level playing field

5 say it to my face

6 stab in the back

7 above board

8 by fair means or foul

Exercise 5

1 a level playing field

2 fair and square

3 not beat about the bush

4 to his face

5 come clean

6 moves the goalposts

7 keep your nose clean

8 by fair means or foul

Exercise 6

being direct	not beat about the bush
	lay your cards on the table
	to someone's face
	call a spade a spade
being fair and honest	come clean
	above board
	on the level
	a level playing field
	fair and square
	keep your nose clean
not being fair or honest	stab someone in the back
	move the goalposts
	below the belt

11 Deception

Exercise 1

1 a

2 b

3 b

4 c

5 a

6 b

Exercise 2

1 E

2 D

3 A

4 F

5 B

6 C

Exercise 3

1 B

2 F

3 E

4 A

5 D

6 C

Exercise 4

1 on the fiddle

2 gives the game away

3 keep it under your hat

4 blow the whistle

5 cover his tracks

6 going through the motions

Exercise 5

1 economical with the truth

2 a hidden agenda

3 a white lie

4 pulling your leg

5 go behind my back

6 keep it under your hat

7 led us up the garden path

8 on the fiddle

Exercise 6

lying	a white lie
	pull someone's leg
pretending	a hidden agenda
	go through the motions
hiding the truth	be economical with the truth
	sweep something under the carpet
telling the truth	blow the whistle on someone
	give the game away

12 Anger and irritation

Exercise 1

1, 2, 4 and 5

Exercise 2

1 up

2 through

3 off

4 off

5 in

6 on

Exercise 3

1 H

2 E

3 G

4 B

5 F

6 A

7 D

8 C

Exercise 4

1 Dmitri gave his brother a dirty look for laughing.

2 Virginia's engagement is a sore point with Cynthia.

3 The headmaster gave us hell when he found out what we'd done. *OR*
When he found out what we'd done, the headmaster gave us hell.

4 I'll only tell you if you promise not to blow a fuse.

5 Clara is likely to fly off the handle if you ask to borrow her bike again. *OR*
If you ask to borrow her bike again, Clara is likely to fly off the handle.

6 When Dad discovered the mess he hit the roof.

7 The knowledge that he is guilty of this crime makes my blood boil.

8 I saw Mr Clarke come marching out of the room with a face like thunder.

Exercise 5

1 C

2 F

3 D

4 B

5 A

6 E

Exercise 6

1 makes my <u>blood</u> boil
2 a <u>face</u> like thunder
3 bit my <u>head</u> off
4 hit a sore <u>spot / point</u>
5 flies off the <u>handle</u>
6 drives me up the <u>wall</u>
7 a pain in the <u>neck</u>
8 a filthy <u>look</u>

Exercise 7

1	B	5	C
2	F	6	G
3	A	7	E
4	H	8	D

13 Fear and frustration

Exercise 1

1	b	4	b
2	a	5	a
3	a	6	c

Exercise 2

1	b	4	b
2	a	5	a
3	b	6	b

Exercise 3

1	D	4	F
2	E	5	B
3	A	6	C

Exercise 4

1 on edge
2 jumped out of his <u>skin</u>
3 gave me the creeps
4 frightened out of her <u>wits</u>
5 <u>a bundle</u> of nerves
6 at the end of his <u>tether</u>

Exercise 5

1 jumped out of my skin
2 on edge
3 until I was blue in the face
4 was shaking like a leaf
5 got cold feet
6 red tape
7 the last straw
8 gave me the creeps OR scared/frightened us out of our wits

Exercise 6

sudden fright	frighten the life out of someone jump out of your skin scare someone out of their wits
feeling nervous	a bundle of nerves butterflies in your stomach get/have cold feet
frustration	not get a word in edgeways at the end of your tether

14 Disagreement

Exercise 1

1	shouting	5	kiss
2	bone	6	pick
3	differ	7	throats
4	fight	8	air

Exercise 2

1	E	5	B
2	D	6	G
3	A	7	F
4	H	8	C

Exercise 3

1	C	4	A
2	F	5	E
3	D	6	B

Exercise 4

1 agree to differ
2 fight like cat and dog
3 jump down my throat
4 gave them a piece of my mind
5 cross swords
6 bone to pick with you
7 clear the air
8 in his bad books

Exercise 5

1 My boss had a go at me about my work.
2 We don't see eye to eye about politics.
3 Housework is often a bone of contention in many families.
4 Getting children to do their homework can be a battle of wills.
5 They argue a lot but always kiss and make up.
6 I don't want this discussion to turn into a shouting match.
7 She waited until she found the right moment to clear the air.

8 I was in my teacher´s bad books for not doing my homework.

Exercise 6

1 see eye to eye

2 at one another´s throats

3 jump down my throat

4 a battle of wills

5 give those decision makers a piece of her mind

6 kiss and make up

7 has a bone to pick

8 a bone of contention

15 Success and failure

Exercise 1

1 b	5 a
2 a	6 a
3 c	7 c
4 b	8 a

Exercise 2

1 F	5 T
2 T	6 F
3 T	7 F
4 F	8 F

Exercise 3

1 We're hoping that our team will win the final hands down.

2 It looks like the exporters are likely to go belly-up.

3 All our arrangements for the launch of the new products have gone pear-shaped.

4 A keen young politician who knows the right people can expect to move up in the world.

5 We have to be prepared to go back to the drawing board to fix these serious problems.

6 It was touch and go whether my manuscript would be finished in time.

Exercise 4

1 went pear-shaped

2 hit the nail on the head

3 plain sailing

4 come up in the world

5 hands down

6 touch and go

Exercise 5

1 plain sailing

2 hit the nail on the head

3 went pear-shaped

4 worked like a charm

5 fall flat on my face

6 are fighting a losing battle

7 saved the day

8 brought the house down

Exercise 6

success	come up in the world hit the nail on the head plain sailing win hands down with flying colours work like a charm bring the house down save the day
failure	back to the drawing board be fighting a losing battle fall flat on your face go belly-up go pear-shaped
Neither success nor failure	touch and go

16 Progress

Exercise 1

1 doldrums

2 ground

3 horse

4 track

5 act

6 hold

Exercise 2

1 a	4 b
2 b	5 b
3 a	6 a

Exercise 3

1 B	4 C
2 E	5 F
3 A	6 D

Exercise 4

1 c	4 b
2 a	5 a
3 c	6 a

Exercise 5

1 D	5 E
2 F	6 A
3 H	7 C
4 G	8 B

Exercise 6

1 on the right track
2 in the pipeline
3 light at the end of the tunnel
4 on hold
5 be barking up the wrong tree
6 get our act together
7 losing ground
8 get to grips

17 Expectation

Exercise 1

1	T	4	T
2	F	5	T
3	F	6	T

Exercise 2

1	a	4	a
2	c	5	b
3	b	6	c

Exercise 3

1	in	5	in
2	for	6	on
3	on	7	before
4	in	8	in

Exercise 4

1	B	4	F
2	A	5	E
3	D	6	C

Exercise 5

1 You shouldn't look so surprised as it's been on the cards for a long time.
2 He did not seem to have a prayer of regaining the world title.
3 Long hours are par for the course for doctors who are still training. *OR* For doctors who are still training, long hours are par for the course.
4 I admit that trying to find you by phoning the embassy was a bit of a long shot.
5 I went on the off-chance that they would need more helpers.
6 It's too early in the day to predict which side will win the match.
7 They spent the afternoon building castles in the air.
8 I sense in my bones that everything will be fine.

Exercise 6

1	F	4	G	7	H
2	E	5	D	8	A
3	C	6	B		

18 Trouble and difficulty

Exercise 1

1	foot	5	circle
2	head	6	goal
3	block	7	trouble
4	leg	8	fly

Exercise 2

1	prevent	4	unable
2	stops	5	offended
3	temporary	6	not

Exercise 3

1 It's biting off more than you can chew.
2 teething problems
3 a Catch 22 situation
4 put my foot in it
5 going from the frying pan into the fire
6 stumbling block

Exercise 4

1 Catch 22 situation
2 a vicious circle
3 in over our heads
4 an own goal
5 fly in the ointment
6 bitten off more than you can chew
7 teething troubles
8 asking for trouble

Exercise 5

1 an own goal
2 teething troubles/problems
3 out of / from the frying pan into the fire
4 a leg to stand on
5 for trouble
6 your foot in it

Exercise 6

causing difficulty	a stumbling block the fly in the ointment an own goal bite off more than you can chew put your foot in it
a difficult situation	a Catch 22 a vicious circle in over your head not have a leg to stand on out of the frying pan into the fire

19 Safety and risk

Exercise 1

1 C, E   3 A, D

2 B, F

Exercise 2

1 D   4 A

2 C   5 F

3 B   6 E

Exercise 3

1 a   4 b

2 c   5 a

3 c   6 b

Exercise 4

1 D   4 C

2 F   5 A

3 E   6 B

Exercise 5

1 fire   5 shave

2 hands   6 side

3 clear   7 bet

4 teeth   8 basket

Exercise 6

1 put all your eggs in one basket

2 sticks her neck out

3 skating on thin ice

4 a close shave

5 take your life in your hands

6 the best bet

7 playing with fire

8 a good bet

20 Money

Exercise 1

1 B, E   2 A, D   3 C, F

Exercise 2

1 b   4 c

2 a   5 a

3 a   6 b

Exercise 3

1 D   4 E

2 A   5 C

3 F   6 B

Exercise 4

1 more   4 no

2 more expensive   5 no

3 David   6 yes

Exercise 5

1 He was paid in advance so he should not be out of pocket.

2 He has just lost his job so from now on he will have trouble making ends meet.

3 A family who have a swimming pool in the garden must be rolling in money.

4 It will cost a small fortune to take the whole group on a foreign tour.

5 It seems to me that paying for taxis to get around is money down the drain.

6 The organization has deep pockets and can afford to pay well.

7 We had to pay an arm and a leg for tickets to the cup final.

8 The company hopes to climb out of the red and even make a profit.

Exercise 6

1 B   4 A

2 F   5 C

3 E   6 D

Exercise 7

1 feel the pinch

2 his shoestring campaign

3 in the red

4 a small fortune

5 charge an arm and a leg

6 tightening their belts

7 down the plughole

8 rolling in money

21 Authority and control

Exercise 1

1 head   5 foot

2 neck   6 hand

3 hand   7 arm

4 finger   8 finger

Exercise 2

1 T   4 T   7 T

2 F   5 F   8 T

3 F   6 F

Exercise 3

1 b   3 c   5 c

2 a   4 b

Exercise 4

1 Some parents try to pass the buck to teachers when their children misbehave.

2 It's time you put your foot down about your son's behaviour.

3 He'll do anything you ask because you've got him twisted around your little finger.

4 I'll stop the debate if things get out of hand.

5 Don't let other people call the shots all the time.

6 I'll see if I can pull any strings to get you an interview.

7 The editor of the newspaper has always been a law unto himself.

8 The people in high places did not share his view.

Exercise 5

1 wears the trousers OR calls the shots

2 get out of hand

3 twisting your arm

4 passed the buck

5 go over his head OR put our foot down

6 put his foot down

Exercise 6

being in control	wear the trousers
	call the shots
	on top of something
	have someone eating out of your hand
	put your foot down
using influence	breathing down someone's neck
	twist/wrap someone around your little finger
	go over someone's head
	twist someone's arm
	pull strings

22 Limitations and restrictions

Exercise 1

1 a   **5** b

2 b   **6** c

3 b   **7** c

4 a   **8** b

Exercise 2

1 F   **4** C

2 D   **5** E

3 B   **6** A

Exercise 3

1 Jenny   **4** Arif's

2 Roger   **5** Leo

3 Birgit's   **6** Atsuko

Exercise 4

1 I've got my hands full.

2 dos and don'ts

3 my hands are tied

4 step on someone's toes

5 off limits

6 overstepped the mark

Exercise 5

1 F   **5** H

2 G   **6** E

3 C   **7** B

4 D   **8** A

Exercise 6

1 a <u>fine</u> line

2 overstepped the <u>mark</u>

3 <u>off</u> limits

4 with no <u>strings</u> attached

5 bend the <u>rules</u>

6 <u>dos</u> and <u>don'ts</u>

7 their <u>hands</u> are tied

8 tread on his colleague's <u>toes</u>

23 Loving and liking

Exercise 1

1 spot   **5** home

2 patch   **6** head

3 flame   **7** dreams

4 torch   **8** grace

Exercise 2

1 you are in love with them

2 ordinary

3 no

4 not as good as you

5 they like you

6 they are not as good as you are

Exercise 3

1 b   **4** a

2 b   **5** c

3 c   **6** b

Exercise 4

1 My piano teacher was a lovely woman and I thought the world of her.

2 He has a common-or-garden teaching job but I think he's a genius.

3 A friend of mine fell head over heels in love with a girl he met on holiday.

4 We have a new car that cost a lot of money but frankly, it's nothing to write home about.

5 Do you have a memory of an old flame that is precious to you?

6 It's a good film but it's not a patch on the films that inspired it.

Exercise 5

1 of their dreams
2 saving grace
3 nothing to write home about
4 had a soft spot for
5 old flame
6 thinks the world of
7 not a patch on
8 head and shoulders above

Exercise 6

romantic love	fall head over heels (in love)
	an old flame
	carry a torch for someone
liking or admiring someone or something	have a soft spot for someone
	head and shoulders above someone/something
	think the world of someone
not being very special	common-or-garden
	no great shakes
	nothing to write home about

24 Happiness and sadness

Exercise 1

1 b	5 c
2 a	6 c
3 a	7 b
4 b	8 a

Exercise 2

1 B	4 C
2 D	5 F
3 A	6 E

Exercise 3

1 MAKE
2 TOP
3 OVER
4 FULL
5 DOWN
6 HAVE

Exercise 4

1 down in the dumps
2 not a happy bunny
3 I really get a kick out of them
4 a shoulder to cry on
5 get on top of you
6 made my day

Exercise 5

1 C, E   2 B, D   3 A, F

Exercise 6

1 <u>a shoulder</u> to cry on
2 <u>on top</u> of the world
3 getting on top of <u>me</u>
4 <u>makes</u> your day
5 <u>down</u> in the dumps
6 not a <u>happy</u> bunny
7 <u>full</u> of beans
8 over the <u>moon</u>

Exercise 7

1 a shoulder to cry on
2 long face
3 made my day
4 look on the bright side
5 get a kick out of
6 broke his heart
7 had a whale of a time
8 down in the dumps

25 Health, illness, and death

Exercise 1

1 death	5 life
2 health	6 knock
3 alive	7 wear
4 kick	8 end

Exercise 2

1 The members of the golf club were dropping like flies with food poisoning.
2 The manager was delighted to receive a clean bill of health for his team.
3 In spite of her problems, her music career is alive and kicking.
4 The heart attack was a wake-up call that scared him terribly.
5 She was suffering from stress and was generally under the weather.
6 I was shocked to see that Bill had become a shadow of his former self.

Exercise 3

1 a	3 a	5 a
2 b	4 c	6 b

Exercise 4

1 fighting for his life
2 given a clean bill of health
3 under the weather
4 skin and bone
5 wake-up call
6 it knocked him for a six

Exercise 5

1 <u>dropping</u> like flies
2 <u>shadow</u> of his former self
3 worse for <u>wear</u>
4 at death's <u>door</u>
5 alive and <u>kicking</u>
6 fighting for his <u>life</u>

Exercise 6

being well	alive and kicking
	a clean bill of health
being unwell	under the weather
	the worse for wear
being thin	a shadow of your former self
	skin and bone/s
almost dying	be fighting for your life
	at death's door
dying	end it all
	kick the bucket

Index

The numbers refer to the unit numbers.